Beth Merriman's Cookbook...

FROM
SOUP TO NUTS

Published in Association with *Parade Magazine*

GROSSET & DUNLAP

A NATIONAL GENERAL COMPANY

Publishers · New York

A Castle Books, Inc. Edition
Distributed To The Trade
By Book Sales, Inc.

Foreword

This is a very special kind of cookbook. It takes for granted that you have at least one good general cookbook filled with standard recipes. Instead, this book offers you *favorite* recipes that are off the beaten track.

Whose favorites? The readers of Parade's food page—as proved by correspondence, surveys and such.

Who are these readers? Women of all ages, with the majority in the "young married" group. Many of them have jobs of their own. All of them are busy-busy-busy.

To meet their needs and save their time, our recipes make use of the so-called "convenience foods" wherever possible. Mixes, canned, frozen, semi-prepared and ready-to-serve foods that cut preparation time are artfully combined with other ingredients to make a recipe the cook can call her own.

We like to use the most modern appliances too. Electric blenders and mixers, reliable heat-controlled ovens; electric skillets, saucepans, grills and so on. These appliances are not always specified, but temperatures are always given and time periods specified.

Once in a while we offer our readers a recipe that takes a little longer to prepare, but is so good that it is well worth the effort involved.

So, from the hundreds of recipes in our tested files we have made the selection you find here, of proven favorites. It was difficult—many more were begging for admission. But if you like this first collection well enough, there is sure to be a second volume, one of these days!

Sincerely yours,
BETH MERRIMAN

Contents

I. Soups

"Some like it hot, some like it cold"—we like it either way, depending on the weather.

No need to tell you that the shelves of your supermarket offer an infinite variety of soups—condensed, ready-to-serve, frozen, dehydrated. There is never any reason to skip the soup because you can't think what to have. A walk down the "soup aisle" will give you a dozen ideas in as many seconds.

Prepared soups can cut down on time and effort and add a blend of delightful flavors when you make a kettle of "homemade" soup. Many of the following recipes use prepared soups in this way. And there are some recipes that start from scratch to end up as a kind of soup not yet available at the market.

So begin with any recipe that appeals to you, and go on from there until you've tried them all!

Crabmeat Soup

1 can (11¼ oz.) condensed green pea soup
1 soup can rich milk or light (coffee) cream
2 cans (10¾ oz. each) condensed tomato soup
1 can (6½ oz.) crabmeat
3 tablespoons dry sherry

Combine pea soup, milk and tomato soup in saucepan; blend thoroughly. Add flaked crabmeat and sherry. Cook over low heat, stirring, until hot. *Makes 4 servings.*

Cream of Pumpkin Soup

2 tablespoons grated onion
2 tablespoons butter or margarine
2 cups chicken broth
¼ cup instant mashed potato powder
1 teaspoon salt
¼ teaspoon pepper
¼ teaspoon nutmeg
1 cup milk
1 cup light (coffee) cream
1 cup canned pumpkin
½ cup dairy sour cream

Sauté onion lightly in butter or margarine in large saucepan. Add broth; heat to boiling; remove from heat. Beat in instant mashed potato, salt, pepper and nutmeg until creamy. Combine milk and cream; stir in. Beat in pumpkin. Simmer, stirring often, 15 minutes. Garnish with dairy sour cream.
Makes 6 servings. May be served hot or chilled.

Hearty Winter Bisque

3 cans (10¾ oz. each) condensed Cheddar cheese soup
3 cans (11¼ oz. each) condensed green pea soup
3 cups dairy sour cream
6 cups milk
1 tablespoon Angostura aromatic bitters
1 cup dairy sour cream

Combine all ingredients except sour cream in large kettle. Blend with rotary egg beater. Heat gently, stirring occasionally, to serving temperature. Top with spoonfuls of dairy sour cream.
Makes 15 servings.

Corn Chowder

1 can (1 lb.) cream-style corn
2 cups milk
1 can (10½ oz.) condensed cream of mushroom soup
½ teaspoon salt
¼ teaspoon hot pepper sauce
Paprika

Empty can of corn into saucepan; add milk. Add soup; blend thoroughly. Bring to boiling point over low heat, stirring frequently. Just before serving, stir in salt and hot pepper sauce. Sprinkle each serving with paprika.   *Makes 6 servings.*

Winter Soup

2 quarts water
1 medium onion, quartered
1 tablespoon salt
¼ teaspoon coarse black
    pepper
1½ lbs. beef chuck
2 tablespoons vegetable oil
1 medium onion, sliced
1 garlic clove, minced
1 tablespoon chopped
    parsley

2 stalks celery, sliced
2 cups shredded cabbage
2 cups sliced carrots
1 can (1 lb.) tomatoes
1 can (1 lb.) kidney beans,
    undrained
¼ teaspoon oregano
½ cup pastina
¼ cup grated Parmesan
    cheese

Combine water, quartered onion, salt, pepper and beef in deep kettle. Bring to boil; lower heat; simmer 2 hours. Remove beef; strain stock; measure; add water to make 2½ quarts. Dice beef. Heat oil in skillet; add sliced onion, garlic, parsley and celery; cook 10 minutes over medium heat, stirring frequently. Return diced meat to stock; add contents of skillet, cabbage, carrots and tomatoes. Cover; simmer 1¼ hours. Add kidney beans, oregano and pastina. Cook 15 minutes longer, or until pastina is tender. Stir in cheese; mix well. Serve at once.

Makes 8 to 10 servings.

Avocado Soup

2 cans (11¼ oz. each) con-
    densed green pea soup,
    chilled
2 tablespoons dry sherry

1 large avocado, peeled,
    stoned, and diced
2 tablespoons lemon juice
2 soup cans milk

Blend thoroughly in electric blender about 2 minutes. Serve cold, garnished with slices of avocado and lemon.

Makes 8 to 10 servings.

Manhattan Scallop Chowder

4 tablespoons butter or
    margarine*
1 teaspoon dried thyme
1 cup sliced onions
3 cups diced potatoes
1 cup sliced celery

8 cups hot water
2 teaspoons salt
⅛ teaspoon pepper
2 cans (1 lb. each)
    tomatoes
1½ cups diced carrots

2 lbs. sea scallops, fresh or frozen (thaw, if frozen)

Melt butter in deep kettle. Add thyme and onions; cook, stirring frequently, until onions are tender but not brown. Add potatoes, celery, water, salt and pepper. Cover; simmer 5 minutes. Add tomatoes and carrots. Simmer, uncovered, 1 hour. Halve scallops crosswise; add. Simmer 5 to 10 minutes longer or until scallops are done. Add salt if necessary. *Makes 8 servings.*

*(Or dice ⅛ lb. salt pork; fry until crisp; remove and save pork scraps for garnish; use drippings instead of butter.)

Chilled Cucumber Soup

1 medium cucumber, peeled
1¼ cups water

1 can (10½ oz.) condensed
    cream of chicken soup

Cut chives

Dice cucumber; cook in water until tender (about 10 minutes). Do not drain. Blend in soup. Chill. Garnish with cut chives.
Makes 3 to 4 servings.

Chilled Lobster Soup

3 cups water
½ teaspoon Worcestershire
    sauce
½ cup nonfat dry milk solids
3 tablespoons flour
1 teaspoon salt

⅛ teaspoon pepper
1 tablespoon grated onion
1 can (7 oz.) lobster meat,
    diced
2 tablespoons lemon juice
Cut chives

Pour water and Worcestershire sauce into top of double boiler. Sprinkle nonfat dry milk, flour, salt and pepper over surface of water. Beat with rotary beater only until blended. Cook over boiling water, stirring constantly, until slightly thickened. Stir in onion and lobster meat. Remove from heat. Chill thoroughly. Stir in lemon juice just before serving. Garnish each serving with finely cut chives. *Makes 4 servings.*

Green and White Soup

1 cup chicken broth
1 can (10¼ oz.) frozen con-
    densed cream of potato
    soup

½ cup dairy sour cream
½ cup diced cucumber
1 tablespoon snipped parsley
4 large stuffed olives, sliced

Heat chicken broth and cream of potato soup over low heat until soup is completely thawed; stir now and then. Cool. Beat until smooth with electric blender or rotary beater. Blend in sour cream and cucumber. Chill for at least 4 hours. Garnish with parsley and sliced stuffed olives. *Makes 4 servings.*

Iced Water Cress Soup

1 bunch water cress
2 cans (10½ oz. each) con-
    densed cream of celery
    soup

2 soup cans milk
1 slice onion
6 sprigs parsley
Salt and pepper

Dash of ground cloves

Wash and drain water cress. Combine all ingredients in electric blender. Blend 1 minute or until water cress disappears into smooth greenness. Chill. Garnish with sprigs of water cress and twists of lemon peel. *Makes 6 servings.*

Quick Vichyssoise

3 tablespoons instant minced onion
1 cup light (coffee) cream
2 cups milk
½ teaspoon salt
Few grains pepper
¼ cup instant mashed potato powder
1 can (10½ oz.) condensed cream of chicken soup
2 tablespoons cut chives

Add instant onion to light cream; let stand 10 minutes. Meanwhile, combine milk, salt and pepper. Bring to scalding point; stir in instant mashed potato; cook over low heat, stirring until smooth and slightly thickened. Combine with cream mixture and soup. Cool. Pour into electric blender or bowl of electric mixer. Blend or beat until smooth and creamy. Chill thoroughly. Serve garnished with cut chives.　　　*Makes 6 servings.*

Seashore Soup

Combine 1 can (10¼ oz.) frozen condensed clam chowder and 1 can (10¾ oz.) condensed tomato soup. Heat gently until frozen chowder melts. Add 2 cups milk; blend well. Heat gently to serving temperature; do not allow to boil.

Makes 4 to 6 servings.

Iced Tomato Gumbo

1 can (10½ oz.) condensed chicken gumbo soup
1 can (10¾ oz.) condensed tomato soup
1 soup can water
1 cup thinly sliced cucumber
1 garlic clove, minced
3 tablespoons wine vinegar
1 tablespoon olive oil

Combine all ingredients. Chill thoroughly. Garnish with sprigs of water cress.　　　*Makes 6 servings.*

Spanish Gazpacho

1 large sweet onion, chopped
2 medium cucumbers, peeled
   and chopped
4 large or 6 medium-sized
   tomatoes, peeled and
   chopped (save juice)
1 garlic clove
1 can (4 oz.) pimientos

3 cups chicken broth or
   bouillon
2 tablespoons olive oil
   (optional)
¼ cup red-wine vinegar
1 teaspoon sugar
2 teaspoons salt, or to taste
Ice cubes

Blend onion, cucumbers, tomatoes, garlic and pimientos in electric blender until fairly smooth, or put through food chopper, using fine knife. Add chicken broth, oil, vinegar, sugar and salt. Mix well; chill thoroughly. When ready to serve, place an ice cube in each soup bowl. Ladle in the soup. Serve with any or all of the following accompaniments: garlic croutons (packaged or homemade), diced unpeeled cucumber, chopped parsley, sliced scallions, diced green pepper, chopped sweet onion, peeled and chopped tomatoes. *Makes 6 generous servings.*

II. Main Dishes

There is an old story about a housewife, tired of planning meals, who said she did wish the Lord had seen fit to make a greater variety of "critters!"

We can't do anything about that, but perhaps the recipes that follow will show you lots of new ways to prepare the available meats. And not meats alone, but poultry of all kinds, fish, shellfish and eggs—casseroles, too, and one-dish meals that make serving so easy.

Let's begin with beef, most popular of all meats, and then go on from there.

MEAT

Quick Sauerbraten

4 to 5 lbs. pot roast (chuck, round or rump)
¼ cup vegetable oil
½ cup chopped onion
2 teaspoons salt
2 tablespoons mixed pickling spices

1 cup red wine vinegar
3 cups water
½ cup firmly packed brown sugar
12 gingersnaps, crumbled

Brown pot roast slowly on all sides in oil in heavy kettle or Dutch oven. Pour off excess oil. Add next 6 ingredients. Simmer 3 to 4 hours, or until tender. Remove meat; keep warm. Strain liquid left in kettle; measure 4 cups. Add gingersnaps.

Cook and stir until smooth and slightly thickened. (If a thicker gravy is desired, stir in 3 tablespoons flour blended with ⅓ cup cold water.) Cook, stirring often, 5 minutes longer .

Burgundy Beef

2 lbs. beef round, cut 1-inch thick
Instant meat tenderizer
1 garlic clove
3 medium onions, sliced thin
4 tablespoons butter or margarine
2 cans (10¾ oz. each) beef gravy
Salt and pepper to taste
¼ teaspoon marjoram
¼ teaspoon oregano
½ cup Burgundy wine
½ pint dairy sour cream

Cut beef into 1-inch cubes; treat with instant meat tenderizer as directed on package. Sauté garlic and onions in butter slowly until onions are soft and lightly browned; discard garlic; remove onions from pan. Brown meat cubes slowly in drippings left in pan. Add beef gravy, salt and pepper. Return onions to pan; simmer 1 hour or until beef is tender. Add herbs and wine; simmer 15 minutes longer. Stir in half the sour cream. Turn into serving dish; garnish with remaining sour cream. Serve with rice or noodles. *Makes 6 servings.*

Beef Stroganoff

3 Bermuda onions
2 lbs. top round steak
1 lb. mushrooms
1 cup butter or margarine
1 can (10¾ oz.) condensed tomato soup
1 can (6 oz.) tomato paste
1 cup dairy sour cream
1 teaspoon salt
Few grains pepper
1 teaspoon Worcestershire sauce

Put onions through food chopper, using coarse knife; then drain, saving juice. Cut meat in very thin slices; trim off excess fat. Slice mushrooms. Brown meat and mushrooms in butter or margarine. Add onions; remove from heat. Combine soup, tomato paste, sour cream, seasonings and onion juice; add to meat mixture. Cover; simmer 1 hour. Serve in ring of fluffy rice. *Makes 6 servings.*

Oven Beef Vegetable Stew
[cover illustration]

1½ lbs. top round, cut into
   1½-inch cubes
2 tablespoons seasoned flour
2 tablespoons vegetable oil
½ cup hot water
1 can (8 oz.) tomato sauce
2 tablespoons lemon juice

¼ cup sugar
1 bay leaf
2 whole cloves
½ pound small white onions,
   peeled
1 cup cut green beans
½ cup sliced carrots
½ cup sliced celery

Dredge meat in seasoned flour; brown on all sides in oil; place
in casserole. Combine water, tomato sauce, lemon juice, sugar,
bay leaf and cloves; pour into casserole. Cover; bake at 300°
for 1 hour. Add vegetables, continue baking until meat and
vegetables are tender.   *Makes 4 servings.*

Pepper Steak

1½ lbs. beef round, cut
   2-inches thick
¾ teaspoon unseasoned in-
   stant meat tenderizer
3 tablespoons vegetable oil
2 large green peppers, cut in
   1-inch squares
3 scallions (with tops),
   thinly sliced
1½ cups diagonally sliced
   celery

1½ cups water, consommé or
   bouillion
1 tablespoon cornstarch
⅓ cup light molasses
3 tablespoons soy sauce
¾ teaspoon salt
1 teaspoon garlic powder
1½ teaspoons Ac'cent
1½ teaspoons ginger
2 teaspoons lemon juice
4 cups hot cooked rice

Cut beef into paper-thin slices; sprinkle slices with tenderizer
according to package directions. Heat vegetable oil in large
skillet over high heat; add beef slices; cook briefly just until
red color disappears. Add peppers, scallions and celery; cook 3
to 5 minutes, stirring frequently. Blend water with cornstarch;
stir in remaining ingredients except rice. Stir quickly into beef
mixture. Stir constantly until slightly thickened and boiling.
Serve with rice.   *Makes 6 servings.*

Coffee-Flavored Pot Roast

1 package instant meat
   marinade
⅔ cup cold coffee
1 medium garlic clove,
   minced or pressed

¼ teaspoon sweet basil
3 to 4 lbs. beef pot roast,
   (any favorite cut)
1 can (10½ oz.) condensed
   cream of mushroom soup

1 large onion, sliced

Pour contents of package of instant meat marinade into Dutch oven with tight-fitting lid. Add coffee, blend thoroughly; blend in garlic and basil. Place meat in marinade. Pierce all surfaces of meat deeply and thoroughly with fork. Marinate 15 minutes, turning several times. Add soup and onion; blend with marinade. Cook over low heat, turning meat once. When liquid begins to bubble, reduce heat. Cover tightly; simmer until tender, approximately 2 to 2½ hours. Remove from gravy to hot platter. Thicken gravy if desired. Slice meat; serve gravy separately.

Makes 6 to 8 servings.

Summer Meat Loaf

1 pound lean beef, ground
½ pound ground pork
½ pound ground veal
½ cup wheat germ
2 eggs
1 medium onion
1 clove garlic
1 teaspoon salt

⅛ teaspoon ground pepper
2 tablespoons catchup
1 teaspoon Worcestershire
   sauce
Dash hot pepper sauce
1 bay leaf
¼ teaspoon thyme
6 strips bacon

Combine ground meats in large mixing bowl. Stir in wheat germ. Place all other ingredients, except bacon, in electric blender; liquefy*. Pour liquid over meat; knead with fingers until well blended. Place 3 strips bacon in bottom of lightly greased loaf pan (8½ x 4½ x 2⅝ inches). Put meat loaf mixture in pan, patting down. Place 3 strips of bacon lengthwise across top. Bake at 350° for 1½ to 1¾ hours or until meat is cooked through.

Makes 6 to 8 servings.

*(If electric blender is not available, use a mortar and pestle after chopping onion and crushing garlic.)

Cape Cod Pot Roast

2 tablespoons vegetable oil
4 to 5 lbs. beef chuck, boned and rolled
½ cup seasoned flour (salt and pepper added)

1 cup fresh cranberries
4 cups water
3 tablespoons brown sugar
¼ teaspoon nutmeg

Heat oil in large kettle; dredge beef with seasoned flour; brown well on all sides. Add cranberries and water. Bring to a boil. Cover; simmer 3 hours or until beef is tender. Strain gravy; measure; thicken with flour mixed to a smooth paste with equal amount of cold water, using 1 tablespoon flour for each cup liquid. Add brown sugar and nutmeg; stir over low heat until sugar dissolves. Season to taste with salt and pepper.

Matchless Meat Loaf

3 tablespoons light molasses
3 tablespoons prepared mustard
3 tablespoons vinegar
4 tablespoons catchup
1 cup milk
2 eggs

1 envelope dehydrated onion soup mix
3 cups soft bread crumbs
½ teaspoon hot pepper sauce
1 teaspoon Ac'cent
½ teaspoon leaf oregano
¼ cup finely chopped parsley

3 lbs. lean beef, ground

Blend molasses and mustard in large bowl. Stir in vinegar, catchup, milk, eggs, onion soup mix and bread crumbs. Stir to mash crumbs. Add remaining ingredients; mix well. Pack into greased loaf pan, 9 x 5 x 3 inches. Bake at 350° for 1½ hours.

Makes 8 servings.

Oatmeal-Raisin Meat Loaf

1 lb. lean beef, ground
1 cup rolled oats, quick or old fashioned, uncooked
½ cup chopped onion
1½ teaspoons salt

⅛ teaspoon pepper
1 teaspoon prepared mustard
1 egg, beaten
1½ cups milk

1 cup seedless raisins

Measure all ingredients into mixing bowl; mix well. Pack firmly in small greased loaf pan. Bake at 375° for about 1 hour. Serve hot or cold. *Makes 6 servings.*

Frosted Meat Loaf

2 lbs. lean beef, ground
2 cups soft bread crumbs
2 eggs
1 teaspoon salt
1 tablespoon prepared
    mustard
¼ cup well-drained prepared
    horseradish

1 large onion, minced
1 teaspoon oregano
1 tablespoon Worcestershire
    sauce
2 tablespoons chili sauce
3 cups hot, well-seasoned
    mashed potatoes

Combine all ingredients except potatoes. Mix thoroughly. Pack into greased 9-inch pie pan. Bake at 350° for 45 minutes. Just before serving top with hot, mashed potatoes. Cut in wedges to serve. *Makes 6 to 8 servings.*

Layered Meat Loaf

4 cups soft bread crumbs
1 small onion, grated
2 teaspoons poultry seasoning
½ teaspoon salt
    Few grains pepper

½ cup melted butter or
    margarine
    Hot water
2 lbs. lean beef, ground
½ teaspoon salt
    Few grains pepper

1 egg

Combine first 6 ingredients; mix well. Add enough hot water to hold ingredients together. Combine remaining ingredients; mix well. Pack half meat mixture in greased 9 x 5 x 3-inch loaf pan. Add bread crumb mixture. Top with remaining meat mixture. Bake at 375° for 1 hour. *Makes 8 servings.*

Sweet and Pungent Meat Balls

3 large green peppers
1 lb. ground beef, seasoned
    with salt and pepper
1 egg, beaten
2 tablespoons flour
1½ teaspoons salt, divided
    Few grains pepper
¼ cup vegetable oil

1 cup chicken bouillon,
    divided
4 slices canned pineapple,
    diced
12 Maraschino cherries
3 tablespoons cornstarch
2 teaspoons soy sauce
½ cup vinegar

½ cup light corn syrup

Cut green peppers in sixths. Form seasoned beef into 16 small balls. Combine egg, flour, ½ teaspoon salt and pepper; dip meat balls in this batter. Heat vegetable oil; add remaining salt. Fry meat balls in hot oil, turning to brown on all sides. Remove meat balls; drain off all but 1 tablespoon oil. Add ⅓ cup bouillon, diced pineapple, cherries and green peppers; simmer 10 minutes. Blend cornstarch, soy sauce, vinegar, corn syrup and remaining bouillon. Add to pineapple mixture; cook slowly, stirring, until thickened. Pour over meat balls. *Makes 4 servings.*

Steak Patties U. S. A.

2 lbs. lean beef, ground
2 teaspoons salt
½ teaspoon pepper
1 teaspoon Worcestershire
    sauce
1 tablespoon steak sauce

¼ teaspoon hot pepper sauce
1¼ cups finely chopped
    onions
3 cups shredded sharp
    Cheddar cheese (¾ lb.)

Combine beef, salt, pepper and sauces; mix well. Shape into 8 patties. Broil 3 inches from source of heat for 8 to 10 minutes, turning once to brown both sides. Top each patty with onions and cheese. Return to broiler long enough to soften cheese. Serve between toasted bun halves.   *Makes 8 servings.*

Stuffed Burgers With Mustard Sauce

1½ lbs. lean beef, ground
1¼ teaspoons salt, divided
2 tablespoons butter or
    margarine
½ cup finely diced celery
3 tablespoons chopped
    onion

1 cup soft bread cubes
⅓ cup wheat germ
1 tablespoon chopped parsley
¼ teaspoon dry mustard
1 tablespoon water

Combine beef and 1 teaspoon salt. Shape into 8 thin patties. Melt butter in skillet. Add celery and onion. Sauté until onion is soft. Add remaining ingredients, including ¼ teaspoon salt, mixing well. Spread stuffing on 4 patties. Top with remaining patties. Broil 4 inches from heat for 10 to 12 minutes, or until done as desired, turning once. Serve hot with mustard sauce.
Makes 4 servings.

MUSTARD SAUCE:

3 tablespoons butter or
    margarine
3 tablespoons flour
¾ teaspoon salt
¼ teaspoon sugar

¾ teaspoon dry mustard
½ teaspoon paprika
½ teaspoon prepared
    horseradish
1½ cups milk

Melt butter in saucepan. Blend in flour and seasonings. Add milk gradually, stirring over medium heat until thick and smooth.   *Makes 4 servings.*

Saucy Meat Balls

MEAT BALLS:
1½ lbs. lean beef, ground
¾ cup rolled oats, quick or
    old fashioned, uncooked
¼ cup chopped onion
1 teaspoon salt
¼ teaspoon oregano
¼ teaspoon pepper
1 egg
½ cup milk

SAUCE:
½ cup chopped onion
⅓ cup chopped green pepper
1 can (1 lb.) tomatoes
1 can (8 oz.) tomato sauce
½ teaspoon salt
¼ teaspoon garlic powder
Dash cayenne
¼ teaspoon oregano
1 bay leaf

For meat balls, combine all ingredients thoroughly. Shape to form 12 meat balls. Brown in just enough vegetable oil to cover bottom of large skillet. Remove meat balls. For sauce, lightly brown onion and green pepper in drippings. Add remaining ingredients; simmer over low heat 15 minutes. Add meat balls to sauce; cover; simmer about 30 minutes. Remove bay leaf. Serve with hot buttered noodles. *Makes 6 servings.*

Barbecued Hamburgers

1 cup bread crumbs
½ cup milk
1 lb. bottom round, ground
1 medium onion, finely
    chopped
¼ cup vegetable oil

½ teaspoon salt
Few grains pepper
¼ cup Worcestershire sauce
2 tablespoons vinegar
¼ cup sugar
1 cup catchup

Combine bread crumbs, milk, meat and onion. Mix well. Form into 12 cakes. Brown on both sides in oil. Combine remaining ingredients; pour over meat cakes. Cover; cook 10 minutes.
Makes 6 servings.

Parmesan Meat Balls With Mushroom Sauce

1 lb. lean beef, ground
1 egg
¼ cup fine, soft bread crumbs
2 tablespoons grated Parmesan cheese
1 teaspoon salt

2 tablespoons butter or margarine
1 can (10½ oz.) condensed cream of mushroom soup
⅓ cup dry sherry
½ cup water

2 tablespoons minced parsley

Combine beef, egg, crumbs, cheese and salt; mix well. Take up mixture by rounded teaspoons; shape into balls. Melt butter in large, heavy skillet; add meat balls, brown on all sides. Pour off all but about 1 tablespoon drippings. Blend mushroom soup, sherry, water and parsley into drippings. Pour over meat balls. Cover; simmer 20 minutes. Stir occasionally during cooking, adding a little more water if sauce is too thick. Serve with broad noodles. *Makes 4 servings.*

Barbecued Veal

1 pound boneless veal
½ pound cooked ham
¼ pound bacon
2 tablespoons vegetable oil
1 cup large stuffed olives
1 medium-sized tomato, cut in wedges
1 cup cooked or canned small white onions

1 medium-sized green pepper, cubed
½ pound mushrooms
¼ cup vegetable oil
½ teaspoon paprika
¼ teaspoon salt
⅛ teaspoon pepper

Cut veal, ham and bacon into 1½ x ½-inch pieces. Heat 2 tablespoons oil; add veal; cook until lightly browned on all sides. Arrange meats, olives, tomato, onions, green pepper and mushrooms on skewers in any desired combination. Combine remaining ingredients; blend. Arrange skewers on broiling rack. Brush with oil mixture. Broil 3 to 4 inches from source of heat 10 minutes, or until lightly browned. Turn; brush with oil mixture several times during the remaining broiling period (about 10 minutes). *Makes 4 to 6 servings.*

Veal Goulash

1½ lbs. boneless veal
¼ cup flour
1 teaspoon salt
Dash pepper
¼ cup chopped onion

1 teaspoon paprika
½ cup vegetable oil
2 medium tomatoes
½ cup hot water
½ cup dairy sour cream

Cut veal in 1-inch cubes. Dredge with flour mixed with salt and pepper. Cook onion, veal cubes and paprika in oil until meat is well browned, stirring frequently. Cut tomatoes into small pieces, add hot water and rub through sieve. Add to meat; cover; simmer 1½ hours or until veal is tender. Add sour cream; simmer 15 minutes longer. More paprika may be added to taste. Serve with buttered noodles. *Makes 4 servings.*

Fruited Lamb Chops

6 canned Bartlett pear halves
¼ cup syrup, drained from pears
¼ cup orange marmalade

¼ teaspoon ground ginger
6 lamb chops
2 unpeeled oranges, cut into 6 thick slices

Parsley

Drain pears. Heat pear syrup, marmalade and ginger until marmalade melts. Broil lamb chops, 4 inches below heat, for about 10 minutes. Arrange pear halves and orange slices on broiler pan. Turn lamb chops. Brush chops and fruits with hot sauce and broil until lamb chops are done, basting occasionally with sauce. Garnish with parsley. *Makes 6 servings.*

Swedish Lamb

8 lamb shanks
4 peppercorns
1 bay leaf

5 fresh dill sprays or ½ teaspoon dried dillweed
Dill Sauce (below)

Cover lamb shanks with measured boiling water. Add 1 tablespoon salt for each quart of water used. Add peppercorns, bay leaf and dill. Cover; simmer 1 hour or until lamb is tender.

Drain; reserve 1½ cups of the broth for preparing the sauce. To serve, arrange lamb shanks on serving dish and pour Dill Sauce evenly over them. Garnish with fresh dill.

Makes 4 generous servings.

DILL SAUCE:

3 tablespoons butter or margarine
3 tablespoons flour
1½ cups hot broth
½ cup milk

2 tablespoons chopped fresh dill or 2 teaspoons dried dillweed
2 tablespoons vinegar
2 teaspoons sugar
Salt to taste
1 egg yolk, slightly beaten

Melt butter; blend in flour. Combine broth and milk; stir in gradually; cook and stir over medium heat until smooth and thickened; simmer 10 minutes. Add dill, vinegar, sugar and salt. Pour a little of the hot sauce on egg yolk; return to remaining sauce; blend. Heat, stirring, for 1 minute (do not boil).

Makes about 2 cups sauce.

Springtime Stew

2 pounds boneless lamb, cut in chunks
2 tablespoons flour
2 teaspoons salt
¼ teaspoon pepper
2 tablespoons vegetable oil
1 garlic clove, minced
1 onion, minced
½ cup thinly sliced celery
2 cups water
1½ teaspoons sugar

6 carrots, cut in 1-inch chunks
8 small white onions, peeled
4 potatoes, pared and quartered
1 package (10 oz.) frozen lima beans
1 tablespoon snipped fresh dill or 1 teaspoon dried dillweed
¼ cup dry, white wine

Roll lamb in mixture of flour, salt and pepper; brown in hot oil. Add garlic, onion and celery; brown lightly. Add water and sugar. Simmer, covered, 1 to 1½ hours or until lamb is tender. Add carrots, onions and potatoes; simmer, covered, about 30 minutes; add more water if necessary. Add lima beans and dill; cook 15 minutes longer, or until all vegetables are tender. Stir in wine; thicken gravy, if desired; heat to serving temperature.

Makes 4 servings.

Ragout of Spring Lamb

3 tablespoons butter or margarine
2½ lbs. boneless shoulder of lamb, cubed
½ teaspoon sugar
1½ tablespoons flour
3 cups lukewarm water
1½ cups consommé

1 large onion, studded with cloves
1 bay leaf
Pinch of thyme
¾ teaspoon salt
¼ teaspoon pepper
½ cup dry red wine
Herb Dumplings (see below)

Melt butter in Dutch oven or large, heavy saucepan. Add lamb, brown on all sides. Add sugar; cook 3 minutes, stirring constantly. Pour off fat. Sprinkle meat with flour; cook until brown, stirring constantly. Stir in water and consommé. Add onion, bay leaf, thyme, salt and pepper. Bring to boil. Cover; simmer 2 hours. Remove onion and bay leaf. Add wine; bring to boil. Drop dumpling dough from spoon on pieces of meat. Cook uncovered over low heat 10 minutes. Cover; cook 10 minutes longer. (Liquid should just bubble gently.) If desired, remove dumplings; keep warm; thicken gravy with 1 tablespoon cornstarch blended with 2 tablespoons cold water.

Makes 6 servings.

HERB DUMPLINGS:

2 cups biscuit mix
¾ cup milk

1 teaspoon each poultry seasoning, instant minced onion, celery flakes and parsley flakes

Combine all ingredients; mix thoroughly with fork. Proceed as directed above. *Makes 12 dumplings.*

Roast Lamb Supreme

1 leg of lamb
2 garlic cloves

1 cup Burgundy wine, divided

Cut slits ½-inch long and ¼-inch deep along length of the leg of lamb; spacing them about 1-inch apart. Peel garlic cloves; cut in fourths, lengthwise. Insert garlic in slits. Place lamb on rack in open roaster. Insert meat thermometer in thickest part of lamb, being sure it does not touch the bone. Roast at 350° for 1 hour. Remove garlic. Baste with ¼ cup wine. Return to oven; roast until done, calculating 30 minutes per pound or until meat thermometer registers 180°. Baste 3 times during remaining roasting period, using ¼ cup wine each time.

Spring Lamb Casserole

1 medium onion, finely
  chopped
1 medium green pepper,
  minced
1 garlic clove, crushed
Pinch of thyme
¼ teaspoon rosemary

½ teaspoon dillweed
3 tablespoons butter or
  margarine
4 shoulder lamb chops
1 teaspoon salt
1 package (5¾ oz.) scalloped potato mix

Combine onion, green pepper, garlic and herbs. Cook in butter or margarine until onion is soft but not brown. Remove onion mixture from pan. Sprinkle chops with salt; brown slowly on both sides in drippings left in pan. Prepare scalloped potato mix as directed on package, using shallow 1½-quart baking dish. Arrange lamb chops on top. Divide onion mixture in 4 equal parts; mound on chops. Bake at 350° for 30 to 35 minutes or until potatoes are golden brown and tender.

Makes 4 servings.

Loin of Pork Hawaii

Pork loin, 8 to 10 chops
1 can (1 lb.) pineapple juice
Hot water
8 whole cloves

12 peppercorns
4 to 5 slices canned pineapple
½ cup firmly packed brown
  sugar

Place pork loin in large kettle; add pineapple juice and enough hot water to cover. Add cloves and peppercorns. Bring to boil; lower heat; simmer 2 hours. Let stand in broth until cool enough to handle. Place fat side up in shallow roasting pan. Cut deep slits between chops. Insert a half slice of pineapple in each slit, round side up. Sprinkle with brown sugar. Bake at 375° for about 1 hour or until pork is browned and thoroughly done.

Makes 8 to 10 servings.

Sweet and Pungent Pork Chops

6 to 8 loin pork chops
1 can (13½ oz.) pineapple chunks
1 can (11 oz.) mandarin oranges
½ cup light molasses
½ cup vinegar
½ teaspoon salt
¼ teaspoon ginger
½ teaspoon soy sauce
2 teaspoons cornstarch
1 teaspoon cold water or pineapple syrup
½ green pepper, diced
6 maraschino cherries

Trim excess fat from chops; place on rack in baking pan. Bake at 325° about 1 hour or until thoroughly done. Drain pineapple chunks and oranges; reserve ½ cup of the pineapple syrup. (Reserve remaining fruit syrup for future use in fruit drinks, punches, etc.) Combine molasses, vinegar and ½ cup reserved pineapple syrup in saucepan. Stir in salt, ginger and soy sauce. Blend cornstarch and cold water until smooth; add to molasses mixture. Add green pepper. Place over medium heat. Bring to boil; stir and simmer 5 minutes. Add pineapple chunks, oranges and maraschino cherries. Simmer 2 minutes longer. Serve over pork chops. *Makes 6 to 8 servings.*

Cajun Pork Chops and Yams

6 pork chops, about ¾-inch thick
4 medium yams
4 cooking apples
⅓ cup orange juice
⅓ cup lemon juice
½ teaspoon cinnamon
¼ teaspoon cloves
2 small bananas

Brown chops on both sides in their own fat. Peel yams; cut each into 3 lengthwise slices. Core apples; do not peel; cut into 12 rings. Arrange yams and apple rings in shallow roasting pan. Top with chops. Combine fruit juices and spices; pour over chops. Bake at 350° for 45 minutes. Cut bananas into thick slices; add. Bake 15 minutes longer. *Makes 6 servings.*

Oven Barbecued Spareribs

3 lbs. spareribs, cut in serving
   pieces
1 teaspoon salt, divided

2 tablespoons Worcestershire
   sauce
¾ cup Basic Barbecue Sauce
   (below)

Place spareribs in shallow baking pan. Sprinkle with ½ teaspoon salt. Add Worcestershire sauce to Basic Barbecue Sauce; brush ribs with part of this sauce. Bake at 350°, brushing frequently with sauce. At the end of 45 minutes turn ribs; sprinkle with remaining ½ teaspoon salt. Brush with remaining sauce. Bake 45 minutes longer. *Makes 4 servings.*

BASIC BARBECUE SAUCE:

1 cup light molasses
1 cup prepared yellow
   mustard

1 cup cider vinegar

Combine molasses and mustard; mix well. Stir in vinegar. Makes 3 cups. (May be stored in covered container in refrigerator.)

Orange-Glazed Ham

1 whole ham (10 to 12
   pounds), fully cooked or
   cook-before-eating type.

Place square of heavy-duty foil in shallow baking pan. Place ham in center of foil, insert meat thermometer through fat side into center of thickest part of ham (do not touch bone). Pull foil up around ham; but do not close tightly. Bake at 325° to 130° internal temperature (about 2 hours) for fully cooked ham and to 160° (about 4 hours) for cook-before-eating ham. Remove from oven about 30 minutes before ham is done; brush with Orange Glaze (below); return to oven. Brush with glaze again in 15 minutes. Remove from oven; let ham stand for 30 minutes.

ORANGE GLAZE:

1 can (6 oz.) frozen orange 2 tablespoons each dry mus-
    juice concentrate,   tard, prepared mustard
    undiluted   and molasses
    1 tablespoon Worcestershire sauce

Blend ingredients in saucepan until smooth; bring to boil. Use
to brush on ham. Serve remaining glaze with ham.

Makes about 1 cup.

Grilled Ham Slice

Select center slice ready-to-eat ham cut 1½- to 2-inches thick.
Slash fat edge at ½-inch intervals. Place on grill or broiler
pan. Combine ½ cup honey, 1 teaspoon Kitchen Bouquet, ¼ cup
lemon juice and ½ teaspoon ground cloves. Brush top of ham
with honey mixture. Grill or broil with surface of meat 5 or 6
inches from source of heat for 5 minutes. Turn; brush with
honey mixture; grill 5 minutes longer. Repeat twice again.

Makes 6 servings.

Ham a la King on Corn Bread Squares

3 tablespoons butter or   4 tablespoons flour
    margarine   ½ teaspoon salt
½ cup thin strips green pepper   2 cups milk
¼ pound mushrooms, sliced   ¼ cup thin strips pimiento
    (about 1 cup)   2 cups diced cooked ham
        Corn Bread Squares

Melt butter or margarine in saucepan. Add green pepper and
mushrooms, cook over low heat until pepper is tender. Add
flour and salt; stir to a smooth paste. Add milk; cook, stirring

constantly until mixture thickens and comes to a boil. Add pimiento and diced cooked ham to sauce. Heat 10 to 15 minutes over very low heat. Serve over hot Corn Bread Squares, made by baking corn muffin mix in a square pan, then cutting into squares. *Makes 4 to 6 servings.*

Barbecued Frankfurters

¼ cup light molasses
¼ cup prepared mustard
3 tablespoons vinegar
2 tablespoons Worcestershire
sauce

¼ cup catchup
¼ teaspoon hot pepper sauce
1 lb. frankfurters

Blend molasses, mustard, vinegar, Worcestershire sauce, catchup and pepper sauce in skillet. Bring to boil over medium heat. Add frankfurters; simmer 10 minutes, turning occasionally. Serve plain or in toasted frankfurter rolls. Spoon any remaining sauce over top. *Makes 8 servings.*

MACARONI FANCY: Spread cut surfaces of hot frankfurter rolls with mustard. Fill roll with canned macaroni and cheese. Top with frankfurter. Sprinkle with minced green pepper and onion. Wrap each in heavy duty aluminum foil. Heat at 350° until piping hot, about 15 minutes.

DUTCH FANCY: Spread cut surfaces of hot frankfurter roll with horseradish mustard, then with pickle relish. Fill with hot sauerkraut; top with hot frankfurter; sprinkle with minced raw onion.

BOSTON FANCY: Brush cut surfaces of hot frankfurter roll with catchup, then with prepared mustard. Fill with hot Boston-style baked beans. Top with hot frankfurter and crisp bacon strip.

Franks and Fettuccini

2 packages (8 oz. each) fet-
tuccini noodles (or me-
dium egg noodles)
16 frankfurters
2 egg yolks
3 cups milk
1 cup whipping cream
4 tablespoons butter or
margarine

4 tablespoons flour
½ teaspoons salt
1 cup Ricotta* cheese
½ cup grated Parmesan
cheese
½ cup grated Romano cheese
2 to 3 tablespoons chopped
parsley

Cook noodles according to package directions; drain. Cut deep
gashes about ½-inch apart along length of frankfurters; broil or
fry until deeply browned. Meanwhile, prepare sauce: Beat egg
yolks slightly; add milk and cream; mix well. Melt butter; blend
in flour and salt. Add milk mixture; stir over low heat until
smooth and thickened. Add cheeses; stir until melted; pour over
hot noodles; toss to mix. Sprinkle with parsley. Arrange with
frankfurters on top. *Makes 8 servings.*

*(Or any dry, fine curd cottage cheese.)

Touchdowners

1 can (12 oz.) luncheon meat
1 cup (¼ lb.) grated American cheese
¼ cup drained pickle relish

1 tablespoon prepared
mustard
2 tablespoons mayonnaise
8 hamburger rolls

Chop luncheon meat. Combine with cheese and pickle relish;
toss lightly. Mix together mustard and mayonnaise; stir into
meat mixture. Spread about ¼ cup of the mixture in each bun.
Wrap each individually in aluminum foil. Bake at 375° for 20
minutes. *Makes 8 servings.*

Apple Bean Bake

2 cans (12 oz. each) luncheon meat
Whole cloves
¼ cup light molasses
3 tablespoons prepared
   mustard

2 tablespoons vinegar or
   lemon juice
2 teaspoons Worcestershire
   sauce
2 cans (1 lb. 4 oz. each) Boston-style baked beans

1 can (20 oz.) pie-sliced apples

Remove luncheon meat from each can in one whole piece.
Score top of luncheon meat; stud with whole cloves. Place
together to form double loaf in center of shallow baking dish.
Combine molasses and mustard in mixing bowl; stir in vinegar
and Worcestershire sauce. Add baked beans and apple slices;
toss. Spoon around luncheon meat. Bake at 350° for 45 minutes.
Makes 8 servings.

Corned Beef Hash Stuffed Peppers

4 large or 6 small green
   peppers
1 can (1 lb.) corned beef
   hash
¼ cup chopped onion
2 tablespoons sweet pickle
   relish

2 tablespoons vinegar
½ cup chili sauce
1 tablespoon brown sugar
1 teaspoon prepared
   mustard
⅛ teaspoon hot pepper
   sauce

Wash peppers; cut slice from stem end of each, remove seeds.
Cover with boiling salted water; cook 5 minutes. Fill peppers
with corned beef hash. Combine remaining ingredients; bring
to a boil. Reduce heat; simmer 5 minutes. Place filled peppers
in casserole; pour sauce over all. Cover; bake at 400° for 30
minutes. *Makes 4 to 6 servings.*

Chili Corned Beef

8 slices bacon, diced
2 medium onions, sliced
2 green peppers, diced
4 cans (1 lb. each) red kidney beans
2 cans (8 oz. each) tomato sauce

¼ cup chili powder
1 teaspoon salt
⅛ teaspoon pepper
2 tablespoons light brown sugar
1 lb. sharp cheddar cheese, grated

2 cans (12 oz. each) corned beef, cubed

Fry bacon until crisp; drain on absorbent paper; set aside. Cook onions and green peppers in 2 tablespoons bacon drippings until onions are soft but not brown. Add kidney beans, tomato sauce, chili powder, salt, pepper and brown sugar; stir to mix well. Add cheese. Cook and stir over low heat until cheese melts. Add corned beef. Heat. Serve on toasted English muffins.

Makes 12 servings.

CASSEROLES AND ONE-DISH MEALS

Scalloped Potatoes and Scallops

2 pounds sea scallops, fresh or frozen
2 packages scalloped potato mix

2 tablespoons butter or margarine
Paprika

Defrost scallops, if frozen. Prepare and bake scalloped potato mix as directed on package. About 15 minutes before end of baking time remove from oven. Arrange sea scallops on top; dot scallops with butter or margarine; sprinkle generously with paprika. Return to oven for remaining baking time.

Makes 6 servings.

Patio Cassoulet

1 medium onion, finely
    diced
½ pound sweet Italian link
    sausage, cut into chunks
2 tablespoons vegetable oil
1 fryer (3½ to 4 lbs.), cut u₁
½ teaspoon salt

1 can (1 lb.) Italian plum
    tomatoes
1 green pepper, cut into
    rings
1 can (1 lb. 4 oz.) white kid-
    ney beans (cannellini)
¼ teaspoon hot pepper sauce

1 teaspoon Worchestershire sauce

Cook onion and sausage in oil in large skillet until sausage is brown; push to one side. Brown chicken pieces in same skillet; remove. Add salt, tomatoes, green peppers to skillet; mix with onion and sausage, cook 5 minutes. Turn into casserole. Add beans, hot pepper sauce and Worcestershire sauce; stir to mix well. Add chicken pieces. Cover; bake at 350° for 45 to 60 minutes, or until chicken is done. *Makes 4 servings.*

Shrimp Jambalaya

1 cup sliced celery
2 cups diced green pepper
2 medium onions, thinly sliced
4 tablespoons butter or marga-
    rine divided
1 or 2 garlic cloves, minced
1 lb. cooked ham, ¾-inch
    thick, cubed

2 lbs. peeled, deveined
    shrimp
1½ teaspoons salt
¼ teaspoon hot pepper sauce
½ teaspoon chili powder
1 teaspoon sugar
2 cans (1 lb. each) whole
    tomatoes

3 cups hot cooked rice

Cook celery, green pepper and onions in half the butter or margarine until tender but not brown; add garlic and ham; cook 5 minutes longer. Add remaining butter, shrimp, salt, hot pepper sauce, chili powder and sugar. Cook, tossing often with fork until shrimp are pink. Add tomatoes; heat. Stir in rice. *Makes 8 servings.*

Stuffed Cabbage Rolls

1 head cabbage
1 lb. lean beef, ground
2 green peppers, chopped fine
2 medium onions, chopped fine
2 tablespoons vegetable oil
1 cup soft bread crumbs
⅓ cup chili sauce

2 teaspoons Worcestershire sauce
½ teaspoon salt
½ teaspoon marjoram
Few grains pepper
1 can (8 oz.) tomato sauce
2 tablespoons butter or margarine
½ cup dairy sour cream

Core cabbage; cook 7 minutes in boiling salted water to cover. Drain; cool; remove 12 large outer leaves*. Meanwhile cook ground beef, green peppers and onions in oil until meat is browned. Add bread crumbs, chili sauce and seasonings; mix well. Place equal amount meat mixture on each cabagge leaf; roll up; secure with wooden picks; place in large skillet; pour in tomato sauce; dot with butter or margarine; cover; simmer about 1 hour. Remove cabbage rolls to platter. Stir sour cream into tomato sauce in skillet. Pour some of this mixture over cabbage rolls; serve remainder separately.   *Makes 6 servings.*

*(Cook remaining cabbage until tender; serve another day, chopped and creamed or in a cheese sauce.)

Tamale Pie

3 tablespoons vegetable oil
1 medium green pepper, diced
1 large onion, chopped
2 pounds lean beef, ground
2 teaspoons Ac'cent
2 teaspoons salt

¼ teaspoon pepper
1 can (1 lb.) tomatoes
1 tablespoon chili powder
1 package (12 oz.) corn muffin mix
1 cup evaporated milk

¾ cup grated sharp cheddar cheese

Heat oil in a 3-quart, heat-proof casserole on top of range. Add green pepper and onion; cook until onion is tender, but not brown. Sprinkle beef with Ac'cent, salt and pepper; brown in casserole, breaking up meat with fork. Add tomatoes and chili powder. Let simmer while preparing topping. Follow package direction for preparing corn muffin mix, omitting egg and substituting 1 cup evaporated milk for liquid called for in directions. Remove casserole from heat; pour corn muffin mixture over top. Sprinkle with grated cheese. Bake at 400° for 20 minutes. *Makes 8 servings.*

Tuna Lasagne

1 can (15½ oz.) spaghetti sauce with mushrooms
1 can (8 oz.) tomato sauce
1 teaspoon oregano
1 tablespoon instant minced onion
1 garlic clove, finely minced (optional)

2 cans (6½ or 7 oz. each) tuna, drained
1 package (8 oz.) lasagne noodles
½ pound Ricotta or any fine-curd dry cottage cheese
½ pound mozzarella cheese, thinly sliced

3 oz. grated Parmesan cheese

Combine spaghetti sauce and tomato sauce; add oregano, minced onion, garlic and tuna. Bring to boil; cover; simmer 15 minutes. While sauce is simmering, cook noodles according to package directions. Spoon about ⅓ of tuna sauce into shallow 2-quart baking dish. Top with half the lasagne noodles, then layer with half the Ricotta cheese and mozzarella cheese slices. Layer with half the remaining tuna sauce and remaining lasagne noodles, Ricotta and mozzarella slices. Top with tuna sauce; sprinkle with Parmesan cheese. Bake at 350° for 40 minutes.

Makes 8 servings.

Quick Baked Beans

4 cans (1 lb. 4 oz. each) Boston-style baked beans
2 medium onions, sliced
⅓ cup light molasses
⅓ cup chili sauce

3 tablespoons vinegar
1 tablespoon Worcestershire sauce
1 teaspoon dry mustard
¼ teaspoon hot pepper sauce

Alternate baked beans and sliced onions in heavy casserole or bean pot. Combine molasses and chili sauce; stir in remaining ingredients. Pour over beans. Bake at 350° for 1 hour.

Makes 12 servings.

Eggplant Patrice

1 small eggplant
4 medium tomatoes, sliced
2 medium green peppers,
   chopped

2 medium onions,
   chopped
Seasoning (salt, pepper,
   garlic salt, Ac'cent)

¾ lb. sharp cheddar cheese, sliced ⅛-inch thick

Slice unpeeled eggplant about ¼-inch thick. Parboil until partially tender. Place layer of eggplant slices in large casserole. Add a layer of sliced tomatoes. Fill spaces with a mixture of green peppers and onions. Sprinkle lightly with each of the seasonings. Add a layer of cheese. Repeat until casserole is filled, ending with cheese. Cover; bake at 400° until steaming (about ½ hour). Remove cover, reduce heat to 350°, cook until eggplant is tender and sauce thick and golden (about ½ hour).

Makes 6 servings.

Empire State Baked Beans

1 pint dried marrow or pea
   beans
3 cups lukewarm water
4 cups cold water (about)
2 onions, sliced
¼ to ½ lb. salt pork, sliced

⅓ cup sugar
¼ teaspoon pepper
1 teaspoon salt
1 teaspoon dry mustard
1 teaspoon paprika

Wash beans; place in large saucepan with lukewarm water; cover. Let stand 12 hours. Do not drain. Add enough cold water to cover the beans well. Slowly bring to a boil; reduce heat; simmer 2 hours. Add water as needed. Add onions and salt pork; cover; simmer until tender (about 2 hours). Transfer to greased shallow 1½-quart baking dish, covering pork with beans. (There should be enough liquid to cover.) Combine remaining ingredients; sprinkle over beans. Bake, uncovered, at 300° until beans are soft and a brown crust forms on top and along sides (3 to 3½ hours). As the beans dry out, moisten with hot water. Beans can be reheated successfully. *Makes 6 to 8 servings.*

Broiled Stuffed Lobster Tails

8 frozen lobster tails (about ½ lb. each)	Few grains turmeric (optional)
⅓ cup butter or margarine	1½ cups milk
2 teaspoons instant green onion	½ cup light (coffee) cream
⅓ cup flour	1 pound shrimp, cooked and peeled
1 teaspoon salt	1 can (7 oz.) minced clams
⅛ teaspoon pepper	¾ cup soft buttered crumbs

Cook lobster tails in water as directed on package. Cool; remove meat, leaving trimmed shells intact. Cut lobster meat in bite-size pieces. Melt butter; add instant green onion; cook 5 minutes over low heat. Blend in flour, salt, pepper and turmeric. Combine milk and cream; add all at once. Cook and stir over medium heat until smooth and thick. Dice shrimp, reserving 8 for garnish; combine with lobster meat. Drain clams; add. Add diced shrimp, lobster and clams to sauce. Refill shells. Sprinkle with buttered crumbs. Broil with surface of food about 4 inches below heat, until golden brown. Decorate tops with whole shrimp; broil a few seconds longer. *Makes 8 servings.*

King Crab Benedict

2 cans (7½ oz. each) Alaska King crab or 2 packages (8 oz. each) frozen Alaska King crab	2 jars (10½ oz. each) Hollandaise sauce
	2 packages (10 oz. each) frozen asparagus
1 tablespoon lemon juice	12 slices toast
3 hard-cooked eggs, sliced	

Drain canned crab or thaw and drain frozen crab. Slice into bite size pieces; sprinkle with lemon juice. Heat Hollandaise sauce; blend until smooth. Add crab. Stir over low heat until serving temperature. Place asparagus spears on toast. Spoon crab mixture over asparagus. Garnish each serving with slices of hard-cooked egg. *Makes 6 servings.*

Shrimp Fiesta

1 bottle or can (12 oz.) beer
  or ale
½ onion
1 sprig parsley
1 lemon wedge
1 bay leaf
1 teaspoon salt
2 pounds raw shrimp, peeled
  and deveined

2 tablespoons butter or
  margarine
2 tablespoons flour
1 can (8 oz.) tomato sauce
4 tablespoons chopped green
  onions (scallions)
¼ teaspoon hot pepper sauce
¼ teaspoon nutmeg
  Pinch sugar

Bring beer, onion, parsley, lemon wedge, bay leaf and salt to boil in kettle. Add shrimp. Bring to boil again; reduce heat; simmer 5 minutes. Remove shrimp. Strain liquid; reserve. Melt butter in skillet; add flour; stir to smooth paste. Add shrimp liquid, tomato sauce, scallions, pepper sauce, nutmeg and sugar. Cook, stirring constantly, until mixture thickens and comes to a boil. Add shrimp; reheat. Serve with hot buttered noodles.
Makes 4 to 6 servings.

Shrimp 'n Rice

1 can (5 oz.) deveined jumbo
  shrimp
1 can (10¾ oz.) condensed
  tomato soup
2 teaspoons parsley flakes
¼ teaspoon garlic powder

½ teaspoon instant minced
  onion
⅛ teaspoon cayenne
¼ teaspoon salt
1 tablespoon butter or
  margarine

1½ cups packaged pre-cooked rice

Drain shrimp; rinse. Measure soup; add enough water to make 1½ cups; heat. Add all remaining ingredients except rice. Bring to boil. Add rice; cover; remove from heat; let stand 5 minutes. Fluff with fork.
Makes 4 servings.

Sardine Rarebit

1 can (10¾ oz.) condensed
    tomato soup
½ cup water
¾ cup non-fat dry milk solids
¼ teaspoon salt

Few grains pepper
¼ pound American cheese,
    grated
4 hard-cooked eggs, halved
1 can Maine sardines

Combine tomato soup and water in top of double boiler. Sprinkle dry milk, salt and pepper over surface. Beat with rotary egg beater until blended; set over hot water. Add cheese; stir until melted. Arrange halved hard-cooked eggs and sardines on platter. Pour tomato cheese sauce over all. Serve with toasted English muffins. *Makes 4 servings.*

Fish Sticks Hawaiian

1 can (1 lb.) sliced
    pineapple
½ cup butter or margarine,
    divided
2 packages (10 oz. each) raw
    frozen breaded fish sticks

1 tablespoon cornstarch
¼ teaspoon salt
½ teaspoon powdered
    rosemary
1 tablespoon lemon juice
3 cups hot, cooked rice

Drain pineapple (save syrup); brown slices lightly on both sides in large skillet in 2 tablespoons butter or margarine; remove from skillet; keep warm. Heat remaining butter or margarine in same skillet; add fish sticks and cook 5 to 6 minutes over medium heat, turning to brown on all sides; remove from skillet; keep warm. Combine cornstarch, salt and rosemary. Combine lemon juice, pineapple syrup and enough water to make 1½ cups; blend into cornstarch mixture; pour into skillet; stir over low heat until thickened. Arrange pineapple slices around platter; add rice; top with fish sticks. Serve sauce separately. *Makes 6 servings.*

Herb-Broiled Halibut

2 pounds halibut steak, fresh or frozen, cut 1-inch thick
⅓ cup butter or margarine
2 tablespoons minced onion
½ teaspoon salt
1 garlic clove, minced

¼ teaspoon coarsely ground black pepper
¼ teaspoon thyme
⅛ teaspoon dried tarragon
¼ teaspoon dried basil
¼ teaspoon dried parsley

1 tablespoon lemon juice

If halibut is frozen, let stand 30 minutes at room temperature. Place halibut in broiler pan without rack, lined with aluminum foil. Cream butter or margarine with onion, seasonings and herbs. Add lemon juice, little by little, mixing thoroughly after each addition. Spread half the herb butter over fish. Broil in preheated broiler, 2 inches below source of heat, 3 minutes for fresh halibut, 5 minutes for partially thawed frozen halibut. With pancake turner, carefully turn fish; spread remaining herb butter over surface. Return to broiler; broil 3 to 5 minutes longer or until fish flakes easily when tested with a fork. (Do not overcook.) Remove to serving platter. Spoon sauce in broiler pan over fish. *Makes 4 to 6 servings.*

Stuffed Fish Fillets

4 to 6 slices bacon, diced
3 to 4 tablespoons bacon drippings
¼ cup chopped onion
¼ cup chopped green pepper
1½ cups water
1 teaspoon salt
½ cup chopped celery
½ teaspoon thyme

Few grains pepper
1½ cups packaged pre-cooked rice
1 cup finely crumbled corn bread or muffins
¼ cup chopped parsley
8 flounder fillets
2 tablespoons butter or margarine
4 lemon slices

Fry bacon in saucepan until crisp. Remove bacon; set aside. Reserve 3 to 4 tablespoons bacon drippings in pan. Add onion and green pepper; cook until tender. Add water, salt, celery, thyme and pepper. Bring quickly to boil over high heat. Add rice. Cover; remove from heat. Let stand 5 minutes. Add corn bread, parsley and bacon; mix lightly with fork. Spread stuffing on 4 fillets. Top with remaining fillets. Place in shallow baking pan. Dot with butter or margarine; top with lemon slices. Add enough water to cover bottom of pan. Bake at 400° for 25 minutes. Serve with Tomato-Lemon Sauce.

Makes 8 servings.

TOMATO-LEMON SAUCE: Brown ¼ cup butter or margarine; add 1 teaspoon each prepared mustard, sugar and Worcestershire sauce, few grains pepper; 1 tablespoon lemon juice and 1 can (8 oz.) tomato sauce. Heat to serving temperature.

Salmon Duo

2 cups diced cooked potatoes
1 can (1 lb.) red salmon, drained and flaked
2 tablespoons chopped onion
¼ cup chopped green pepper
1 hard-cooked egg, chopped
1 teaspoon salt
½ cup mayonnaise or salad dressing
2 teaspoons prepared mustard
2 teaspoons vinegar
⅛ teaspoon hot pepper sauce
2 tomatoes

SALMON SALAD: Combine potatoes, flaked salmon, onion, green pepper and egg; sprinkle with salt. Mix together mayonnaise, mustard, vinegar and hot pepper sauce; add to potato mixture. Mix lightly with a fork, being careful not to break potatoes; chill. Serve on salad greens; garnish with tomatoes, cut in wedges.

SALMON CASSEROLE: Prepare as for salad, but do not chill. Turn into a 9-inch pie plate or shallow casserole. Arrange tomatoes, cut in wedges or sliced, around edge. Bake at 375° for 25 minutes. *Makes 4 servings.*

Rolled Omelet Louisiana

2 tablespoons butter or
   margarine
6 eggs
6 tablespoons water

½ teaspoon salt
Few grains pepper
Shrimp Sauce (below)

Melt butter or margarine in 10-inch frying pan. Beat eggs slightly; add water, salt and pepper. Pour into frying pan. Cook over low heat until eggs set on bottom of pan. Lift edge and tilt pan so that some of the uncooked egg mixture flows under cooked eggs. Repeat until omelet is cooked through and brown on bottom. Top with Shrimp Sauce; loosen with spatula; roll. Turn out on hot platter. *Makes 4 to 6 servings.*

SHRIMP SAUCE: Make 1 cup cream sauce using 4 tablespoons butter or margarine, 3 tablespoons flour, 1 cup milk or light cream, salt and pepper. Add 1 can (5½ oz.) small shrimp, drained.

Fluffy Omelet

3 tablespoons quick-cooking
   tapioca
1 teaspoon salt
⅛ teaspoon pepper
1 cup milk

1½ tablespoons butter
6 egg yolks, beaten thick
6 egg whites, stiffly beaten
Green Pea Sauce (below)

Combine tapioca, salt, pepper and milk in saucepan. Cook over medium heat until mixture comes to a full boil, stirring constantly. Add butter; remove from heat; let cool slightly. Add egg yolks; mix well. Fold egg yolk mixture into egg whites. Turn into hot, buttered, 10-inch skillet or omelet pan; cook over low heat 3 minutes. Bake at 350° for 15 minutes. If skillet is used, run spatula quickly around edge; cut across at right angles to handle of pan, being careful not to cut all the way through. Pour about half of Green Pea Sauce on omelet; fold carefully from handle to opposite side. Serve on hot platter with remaining sauce. *Makes 4 servings.*

GREEN PEA SAUCE: Cook 1 box (10 oz.) frozen green peas as directed. Drain. Prepare 1½ cups well-seasoned medium white sauce. Add peas; heat thoroughly. *Makes 3 cups sauce.*

Easter Eggs Marguerite

8 slices bread
Prepared mustard
8 slices cooked ham

½ lb. package (8 square slices) American cheese
8 eggs, separated

Toast bread slices on one side. Spread untoasted side with prepared mustard, top with 1 slice of ham, then with 1 slice of cheese. Beat egg whites stiff; mound on cheese, making a hollow in center. Slip 1 whole egg yolk into each hollow. Place on greased cookie sheet. Bake at 350° until yolks are set and whites lightly browned. Serve at once.

POULTRY

Hawaiian Chicken

1 broiler-fryer chicken, quartered
1 teaspoon Ac'cent
2 tablespoons vegetable oil
1 medium onion, chopped
1 garlic clove, minced
1 can (20 oz.) pineapple chunks
3 tablespoons soy sauce
1 bay leaf, crumbled
½ cup flaked coconut

1¼ cups water, divided
2 tablespoons cornstarch
1 cup diagonally sliced celery
2 medium tomatoes, peeled and cut in 8 wedges each
1 green pepper, cut in 1-inch pieces
½ teaspoon salt
3 cups hot cooked rice

¼ cup toasted slivered almonds

Sprinkle chicken on both sides with Ac'cent. Brown chicken on both sides in hot oil; remove. Add onion and garlic; cook until tender but not brown. Return chicken to skillet. Add syrup from pineapple, soy sauce, bay leaf, coconut and 1 cup water. Cover; simmer 20 minutes. Blend cornstarch and ¼ cup water; add to skillet; stir constantly until thickened and clear. Add drained pineapple chunks, celery, tomatoes and green pepper. Sprinkle with salt. Cover; simmer 10 minutes. Serve over hot cooked rice. Sprinkle with almonds. *Makes 4 servings.*

Harvest Chicken

2 broiler-fryer chickens, quartered
1½ teaspoons salt
1½ teaspoons Ac'cent
½ cup butter or margarine
1½ cups orange juice
2 tablespoons slivered orange peel*

2 teaspoons instant minced onion
½ teaspoon ginger
¼ teaspoon hot pepper sauce
4 teaspoons cornstarch
2 oranges, sectioned
2 cups seedless grapes
½ cup toasted slivered almonds

Sprinkle chicken quarters on both sides with salt and Ac'cent Heat butter in large skillet. Add chicken quarters 4 at a time; brown on both sides, removing as browned. Return all of chicken to skillet; add orange juice and peel, onion, ginger and hot pepper sauce. Simmer, covered, 30 to 35 minutes, until chicken is tender. Arrange chicken on heated platter; keep warm. Blend cornstarch with a little cold water; stir into sauce in skillet. Cook, stirring constantly, until mixture thickens and comes to a boil. Add orange sections and grapes; heat gently. Add almonds. Pour a little of sauce over chicken; serve remaining sauce separately. Surround chicken with hot mashed potatoes. Garnish with parsley, additional orange sections and small grape clusters.   *Makes 8 servings.*

*(To prepare slivered peel: Wash orange and remove peel (very thin) with vegetable peeler. Cut with scissors or knife into fine slivers.)

Chicken Cacciatore

1 frying chicken (3½ pounds), cut up
½ cup seasoned flour
⅓ cup vegetable oil
1 garlic clove, minced
2 medium onions, chopped

1 green pepper, diced
1 can (1 lb.) tomatoes
1 can (6 oz.) tomato paste
½ lb. mushrooms, sliced
1½ teaspoons salt
¼ teaspoon pepper

¾ teaspoon oregano

Dredge chicken in flour. Brown on all sides in vegetable oil. Add all remaining ingredients except oregano. Simmer for 30 minutes. Add oregano; simmer 15 minutes longer, or until chicken is tender. *Makes 6 servings.*

Chicken Rosemary

1 broiler-fryer chicken, quartered
Seasoned flour
⅓ cup vegetable oil
2 tablespoons butter or margarine
½ cup giblet broth
½ garlic clove, minced
1½ teaspoons salt
Pepper to taste
1 tablespoon rosemary
½ cup dry white wine
1 teaspoon white vinegar

Dredge chicken with seasoned flour; cook slowly in oil and butter until lightly browned. Add garlic, salt and pepper. Continue cooking until chicken is golden brown. Add rosemary, wine, vinegar and broth from giblets. Cover; bake at 350° about 30 minutes or until chicken is tender. *Makes 4 servings.*

Chicken Jambalaya

2 medium onions, minced
1 green pepper, minced
1 garlic clove, minced
2 tablespoons vegetable oil
1 stewing chicken (4 to 5 lbs.), cut up
1 can (8 oz.) tomato sauce
½ cup water
1½ teaspoons salt
Few grains pepper
1 teaspoon chili powder
Boiling water
1½ cups rice (uncooked)
⅓ cup seedless raisins

Cook onions, green pepper and garlic in oil in large kettle or Dutch oven until soft but not brown. Add chicken. Combine tomato sauce, ½ cup water, salt, pepper and chili powder; pour over chicken. Add enough boiling water to cover; cover kettle; simmer 45 minutes. Add rice, simmer 35 minutes longer or until chicken is tender, adding more water if necessary. Add raisins; simmer 10 minutes longer. Sprinkle with grated cheese and minced parsley, if desired. *Makes 6 servings.*

Turkey-Pineapple Curry

½ cup minced onion
⅓ cup butter or margarine
⅓ cup flour
1 tablespoon curry powder
1 teaspoon salt
½ teaspoon Ac'cent

4 instant chicken bouillon
    cubes
3 cups hot water
3 cups diced leftover turkey
1 can (8 oz.) pineapple tid-
    bits, drained

Cook onion in butter until soft but not brown. Blend in flour, curry powder, salt and Ac'cent. Crumble chicken bouillon cubes; add. Add water; cook over low heat, stirring constantly, until thickened. Add turkey and pineapple. Heat to serving temperature. Serve with rice and curry accompaniments: peanuts, chutney, golden raisins and coconut.

Turkey Rarebit

½ cup dry sherry
2 tablespoons minced onion
½ cup diced green pepper
1 cup grated process Ameri-
    can cheese
2 tablespoons flour

1 teaspoon salt
1 cup light (coffee) cream
1 can (6 oz.) broiled sliced
    mushrooms
Leftover turkey, sliced or
    cubed

Toast points

Combine all ingredients except mushrooms and turkey in top of double boiler. Add broth from mushrooms. Stir over hot water until cheese melts and mixture thickens. Add mushrooms. If there is enough turkey to slice, serve sauce separately. If not, cube and add to sauce. Serve on toast points.

Makes enough sauce for 6 servings.

Turkey Supreme

4 cups cooked broccoli
Leftover turkey, sliced

Velvet Sauce (below)
Parmesan cheese, grated

Arrange hot, cooked broccoli in ramekins or 1 large, shallow baking dish; add layer of turkey. Fill dishes with hot Velvet Sauce; dust with grated cheese; place under broiler until top browns; serve at once. *Makes 6 servings.*

VELVET SAUCE:

2 tablespoons butter or
  margarine
2 tablespoons flour
1 teaspoon paprika
¾ teaspoon salt
⅛ teaspoon pepper
1 cup milk

2 cans (10½ oz. each) condensed cream of chicken soup
½ lb. process American cheese, cut in small pieces

Melt butter or margarine; blend in flour and seasonings; add milk gradually, stirring until thickened. Add soup; blend. Add cheese; stir over low heat until cheese melts.
Note: Leftover gravy, or part gravy and part soup (2⅔ cups in all) may be used.

Rock Cornish Hens Grenadine

4 Rock Cornish hens
  Pineapple-Walnut Stuffing
  (below)
¼ cup lemon juice

½ cup honey
¼ cup grenadine syrup
½ cup soft butter or
  margarine

Thaw hens, if frozen. Stuff. Combine lemon juice, honey and grenadine syrup. Set aside ½ cup for basting; blend remainder with butter. Spread over surface of birds. Roast at 350° for about 1 hour or until done, brushing occasionally with honey mixture. *Makes 4 servings.*

PINEAPPLE-WALNUT STUFFING:

½ cup water
¼ cup butter or margarine
½ package bread stuffing mix
  (4 oz.)

1 egg, slightly beaten
½ cup crushed pineapple
¼ cup finely chopped walnuts

Heat water; add butter; heat until melted. Stir in remaining ingredients. *Makes enough to stuff 4 hens.*

Rock Cornish Hens Normandy

3 frozen Rock Cornish hens
1 teaspoon salt
½ teaspoon sage
½ teaspoon nutmeg
½ garlic clove, crushed

2 tablespoons lemon juice
½ cup butter or margarine
½ cup orange juice
3 thick slices unpeeled navel orange

Powdered cloves

Thaw hens; split in half down the middle. Combine salt, sage, nutmeg, garlic and lemon juice; rub over skin side of hens. Melt butter in shallow roasting pan in 350° oven. Place hens, skin side down, in melted butter. Roast 15 minutes. Turn skin side up. Roast 15 minutes longer. Pour orange juice over hens. Roast another 15 minutes or until hens are golden brown and fork-tender. Remove to platter; pour pan juice over all. Garnish with halved orange slices sautéed in a little butter to which a dash of powdered cloves has been added. *Makes 6 servings.*

Pineapple Duckling

1 duckling, 4 to 5 pounds, quartered
2 teaspoons Kitchen Bouquet
2 tablespoons vegetable oil
1 teaspoon salt
½ teaspoon onion salt
½ teaspoon celery salt
½ teaspoon ginger

1 cup canned pineapple juice
2 cups raw carrots, diagonally sliced
1 can (9 oz.) sliced pineapple
2 medium-sized green peppers, cut in eighths
2 tablespoons cornstarch
2 tablespoons cold water

Skin duckling; brush lightly with Kitchen Bouquet. Heat vegetable oil in large frying pan or Dutch oven; add duckling; brown on both sides. Combine seasonings; add. Add pineapple juice and carrots. Cover; cook over low heat until duckling is just tender (about 45 minutes). Cut pineapple slices in eighths; add with green pepper. Cook until green pepper is tender, but still crisp, about 5 minutes. Combine cornstarch and cold water; stir in. Cook, stirring constantly, until sauce thickens and boils. *Makes 4 servings.*

Duckling, Spanish Style

¼ cup vegetable oil
1 tablespoon paprika
1 duckling (4 to 5 lbs.),
   quartered
1 medium onion, thinly sliced
¼ cup flour
½ cup dry sherry

2 cups giblet stock or
   bouillon
1 medium tomato, sliced
¼ cup chopped pimiento-
   stuffed green olives
2 tablespoons minced parsley
Paprika

Combine vegetable oil and 1 tablespoon paprika in large skillet; mix well. Add duckling; cook until browned on all sides; remove duckling. Add onion to drippings; cook 5 minutes. Add flour; mix well. Gradually add sherry and stock or bouillon, stir over low heat until thickened. Add tomato, olives, parsley and duckling. Cover; cook over low heat about 1 hour, or until duckling is tender. Sprinkle with paprika.   *Makes 4 servings.*

Braised Duck Cantonese

1 duck (6 to 7 lbs.)
1 teaspoon salt
1 egg
1 tablespoon water
1 cup flour
2 cups vegetable oil
1 tablespoon minced scallions

Diced duck giblets
1 cup duck broth
2 tablespoons cornstarch
¼ cup water
1 tablespoon soy sauce
1 tablespoon dry sherry
½ teaspoon cinnamon

Have duck disjointed at market. Remove fat. Cover with cold water; bring to boil; cover; simmer 45 minutes or until tender. Remove from broth; cool. Remove bones and skin; cut meat into pieces about 2 inches by ½ inch. Sprinkle with salt. Beat egg slightly; add water. Dip duck first in flour, then in egg, then in flour again. Heat oil in deep frying pan or Dutch oven; add duck; cook over medium heat until golden brown, about 10 minutes; drain. Place on serving platter; sprinkle with scallions. Meanwhile cook diced giblets in broth about 10 minutes. Blend cornstarch and water; add to broth with remaining ingredients. Cook, stirring, until thickened. Pour over duck. Serve with fluffy rice.   *Makes 4 servings.*

III. Salads and Salad Dressings

In a relatively short time salads have raced ahead in popularity until now we rarely plan a meal that does not include one, either as a first course, an accompaniment to the main course, a course by itself, or as dessert.

We like the West coast custom of serving a tossed green salad for the first course. It begins the meal on a fresh, zestful note that seems to stimulate appetite, while a salad served after the main course is often ignored or only partially eaten because the appetite is sated.

Among the recipes that follow you will find salads of all types for your family's enjoyment.

Don't forget the stunning array of salad dressings—from French or Italian to Russian or Green Goddess—available at your supermarket. Some come in attractive bottles, some in packages, needing only the addition of liquid. Keep a few varieties on hand to lend distinctive flavor to salads you concoct.

Cottage Cheese Ring With Fruit

2 envelopes unflavored
   gelatin
½ cup cold water
3 cups creamed cottage
   cheese

1½ cups mayonnaise
2 tablespoons lemon juice
2 tablespoons sugar
Salt to taste

Sprinkle gelatin on cold water; dissolve over hot water; cool slightly. Mix cottage cheese and mayonnaise; stir in dissolved gelatin; mix thoroughly. Add lemon juice, sugar and salt; blend gently but thoroughly. Turn into an oiled 5-cup ring mold; chill until firm. Fill center of ring with mixed fresh fruit. Serve with Banana Dressing. *Makes 8 servings.*

BANANA DRESSING: Mash 2 fully ripe bananas; add ¼ cup mayonnaise. Whip ¼ cup whipping cream; fold in. Or put cut-up bananas, mayonnaise and whipping cream in an electric blender; blend smooth.

Cucumber-Lime Mousse

1 package lime-flavored gelatin
1 cup hot water
2 large cucumbers
1 tablespoon lime juice
1 teaspoon Worcestershire sauce
1 teaspoon salt
½ teaspoon pepper
¼ teaspoon hot pepper sauce
1 tablespoon prepared horseradish
½ cup mayonnaise
2 cups dairy sour cream
Salad greens

Dissolve gelatin in hot water; chill until consistency of unbeaten egg white. Meanwhile peel cucumbers, discard seeds, chop fine (makes about 1½ cups), sprinkle with lime juice. Let stand 5 minutes. Drain thoroughly; add remaining ingredients; blend well. Fold into chilled gelatin. Turn into 5-cup mold. Chill until set. Unmold on salad greens. Decorate top with thin slices of unpeeled cucumber marinated in French dressing.

Makes 6 servings.

Quick Tomato Aspic

2 envelopes unflavored gelatin
½ cup cold water
2 teaspoons sugar
½ teaspoon salt
2 cans (8 oz. each) tomato sauce
2 cups water
Dash hot pepper sauce
1 teaspoon Worcestershire sauce

Sprinkle gelatin on cold water in top of small double boiler; dissolve over hot water. Combine remaining ingredients. Add gelatin; mix well. Pour into 8 to 10 individual molds; chill until set.

Creamy Potato Salad

4 cups sliced hot, cooked
  potatoes
Bottled Italian dressing
1 cup dairy sour cream
¼ cup sliced green onion
2 tablespoons snipped parsley
2 tablespoons chopped dill
  pickle

2 tablespoons diced pimiento
2 tablespoons vinegar
1 tablespoon prepared
  mustard
1 teaspoon salt
⅛ teaspoon pepper
1 cup sliced celery
3 hard-cooked eggs, chopped

Cook potatoes in jackets. Peel and slice while hot. Add a small amount of Italian dressing to coat the warm sliced potatoes. Refrigerate. Combine sour cream with onion, parsley, dill pickle, pimiento, vinegar, mustard, salt and pepper. Add to potatoes, with celery and chopped eggs. Toss gently; chill. Garnish with sliced stuffed olives. *Serves 6.*

Relish Salad

2 envelopes unflavored gelatin
1 cup cold water
1 teaspoon salt
1 cup creamed cottage cheese
1 cup mayonnaise
2 tablespoons prepared
  mustard

¼ teaspoon hot pepper sauce
1 tablespoon grated onion
1 cup pickle relish
½ cup diced green pepper
1 cup chopped cucumber
1½ cups diced celery
¼ cup chopped stuffed olives

Sprinkle gelatin on cold water to soften. Place over boiling water; stir until gelatin is dissolved. Add salt; cool. Put cottage cheese through strainer, or beat on high speed of electric mixer until smooth; add mayonnaise, prepared mustard and hot pepper sauce; gradually add gelatin mixture, stirring until well-blended. Mix in remaining ingredients. Turn into 8 or more individual molds; chill until firm. Unmold; garnish with sprigs of parsley. Serve with assorted cold cuts.

California Salad Bowl

2 heads iceberg lettuce, cut into small chunks
¼ cup Garlic Flavored Vegetable Oil (below)
½ cup plain vegetable oil
1 tablespoon Worcestershire sauce
Salt and pepper to taste

½ cup grated hard cheese, such as Romanelle
¼ cup crumbled blue cheese
½ teaspoon dry mustard
⅓ cup lemon juice
1 egg
Toast Croutons (below)

Combine all ingredients in large salad bowl. Toss until lettuce is coated with oils, egg, seasonings and cheese. Dip Toast Croutons in additional Garlic-Flavored Oil; drain; add to salad just before serving.   *Makes 8 large servings.*

GARLIC-FLAVORED VEGETABLE OIL: Cut 4 garlic cloves into 1 cup salad oil; let stand for several hours until oil is well-flavored. Remove garlic. Save any unused oil for another time.

TOAST CROUTONS: Cut bread slices into ½-inch cubes; measure 2 cups. Toast at 350° until golden brown and crisp, stirring often to make sure that all cubes are evenly browned.

Molded Garden Salad

1 envelope unflavored gelatin
½ cup cold water
¾ cup hot water
¼ cup sugar
½ teaspoon salt
¼ cup mild vinegar

2 tablespoons lime juice
12 thin slices unpeeled cucumber
¾ cup thinly sliced radishes
¼ cup thinly sliced scallions
½ cup diced celery

Lettuce

Soften gelatin in cold water. Add hot water, sugar, and salt; stirr until gelatin and sugar dissolve. Add vinegar, and lime juice. Chill until consistency of unbeaten egg whites. Stir in cucumber, radishes, scallions, and celery. Spoon into 1 large or 6 individual molds; chill. Serve on lettuce with mayonnaise.   *Makes 6 servings.*

Old Fashioned Cole Slaw

⅓ cup sugar
½ teaspoon dry mustard
¼ teaspoon salt
Few grains pepper
1 egg

⅓ cup milk
⅓ cup vinegar
1 tablespoon butter or
margarine
3 cups shredded cabbage

Paprika

Combine sugar, mustard, salt and pepper. Beat egg; add with milk; mix well. Add vinegar slowly. Cook, stirring constantly, until mixture boils. Add butter or margarine; stir until melted. Chill. Toss dressing with shredded cabbage; sprinkle with paprika. *Makes 6 servings.*

Macaroni Ham Salad

2 cups (8 oz.) elbow
macaroni
1 pound cooked ham, ½-inch
thick
1 cup sliced celery
1 medium green pepper,
chopped
¾ cup sliced pitted black
olives

⅓ cup prepared mustard
½ cup whipping cream
⅓ cup minced onion
1 tablespoon prepared
horseradish
1 teaspoon salt
½ teaspoon garlic salt
½ teaspoon pepper
Crisp salad greens

2 cups cherry tomatoes

Cook macaroni according to package directions. Drain in colander. Rinse with cold water; drain. Cut ham in ½-inch cubes; combine with macaroni, celery, green pepper and olives; toss to mix. Combine mustard, cream, onion, horseradish, salt, garlic salt and pepper; mix well. Add dressing to macaroni mixture; toss well. Chill. Serve on salad greens, garnish with cherry tomatoes. *Makes 6 to 8 servings.*

Salmon Potato Salad

1 cup pitted ripe olives
1 can (8 oz.) red salmon
2 cups diced cooked potatoes
½ cup diced cucumber
1 small onion, thinly sliced
Salad greens

½ cup dairy sour cream
1 teaspoon salt
2 tablespoons cider vinegar
Freshly ground black pepper

Slice olives. Drain salmon, remove skin and bones; break into large pieces. Combine olives, salmon, potatoes, cucumber and onion. Chill. Blend sour cream, salt, vinegar and pepper. Add to salmon mixture; mix lightly. Serve on crisp salad greens.

Makes 4 to 6 servings

Chef's Salad

1 head romaine lettuce
1 bunch water cress
1 cucumber
1 bunch radishes

¼ lb. cooked ham
¼ lb. Swiss cheese
6 small tomatoes
8 large stuffed olives

Wash romaine and water cress; drain; put in covered vegetable crisper in refrigerator. Pare cucumber; score lengthwise with tines of fork; slice into ice water. Make radish roses; drop into ice water. Cut ham and cheese in thin strips. Cut tomatoes in wedges. Slice olives. Put greens in salad bowl. Arrange remaining ingredients in attractive pattern on greens. Just before serving, toss with Onion French Dressing.

Makes 6 to 8 servings

ONION FRENCH DRESSING: Combine ½ cup vegetable oil, 3 tablespoons vinegar, ¾ teaspoon salt, 2 teaspoons sugar, ¼ teaspoon dry mustard, ½ teaspoon paprika, few grains pepper and 2 tablespoons minced onion. Let stand ½ hour. Shake well before using. *Makes about ¾ cup dressing.*

Savory Potato Salad

6 medium potatoes, cooked
    and peeled
1 cup sliced celery
2 tablespoons minced parsley

Salt and pepper
6 strips bacon
¼ cup cider vinegar
1 tablespoon sugar

Cut potatoes in thin slices. Add celery, parsley, salt and pepper.
Cut bacon in 1-inch pieces; fry until crisp; add vinegar and
sugar to bacon and drippings; heat; pour over potato mixture;
toss gently to mix. Cover; let stand over low heat until warm.
Makes 6 servings.

Tuna, Rice and Pineapple Salad

⅔ cup packaged precooked
    rice
½ teaspoon salt
⅔ cup boiling water
1 can (6½ or 7 oz.) tuna,
    drained
½ cup diced celery

1 package (12 oz.) quick-
    frozen pineapple chunks,
    defrosted or 1 can (1 lb.)
    pineapple chunks
¾ cup mayonnaise or salad
    dressing
1 tablespoon lemon juice

Salad greens

Add rice and salt to rapidly boiling water. Cover; remove from
heat. Let stand 5 minutes; fluff with fork. Cool. Break tuna into
fairly large pieces; add with celery. Add well-drained pineapple
and remaining ingredients. Toss lightly to mix. Chill 1 hour. Serve
on salad greens. *Makes 4 servings.*

IV. Breads

In recent years there has been a great resurgence of interest in making yeast breads at home. Not enough bread to meet the needs of every day, of course. There is no necessity for that, with the wonderful variety of ready-baked bread and rolls, the brown 'n serve products and the refrigerated doughs —ready to bake into delicious croissants, sweet rolls, and the like. But our readers have told us that every so often they like to bake a loaf or two of their very own.

We must admit that the whole process of bread-making is fascinating and that the aroma of baking bread is sheer heaven. Reasons enough!

Batter breads are time-savers and this new way to make yeast breads has proved very popular with our readers.

Quick breads have always been popular and how they do dress up an ordinary meal! Now some are quicker than quick, with a mix used as a base. You will find many such among the recipes that follow.

4-Way Nut Bread

½ cup sugar	1¼ cups milk
1 egg	1½ cups chopped nuts
	3 cups biscuit mix

Mix together sugar, egg, milk and nuts. Stir in biscuit mix. Pour into well-greased 9 x 5 x 3-inch loaf pan. Bake at 350° for 45 to 50 minutes. Remove from pan to rack. Cool thoroughly before slicing.

APRICOT ALMOND BREAD: Follow directions for 4-Way Nut Bread but use apricot nectar instead of milk, and instead of chopped nuts, ¾ cup canned roasted and diced almonds and 1 cup chopped dried apricots.

BANANA WALNUT BREAD: Follow directions for 4-Way Nut Bread but use ¾ cup sugar and only ½ cup milk; use only ¾ cup chopped walnuts and add 1 cup mashed bananas (2 to 3 fully ripe bananas).

LEMON-PECAN BREAD: Follow directions for 4-Way Nut Bread but use 1 cup sugar; instead of milk, use 1 cup water, plus ¼ cup lemon juice, plus 1 tablespoon grated lemon peel. Use only ¾ cup chopped pecans. Stir in 2 tablespoons melted shortening or vegetable oil.

Versatile Pancake Mix

COFFEE CAKE: Beat 1 cup sugar into 1 beaten egg. Add, alternately, 1 cup pancake mix, ½ cup milk. Add 3 tablespoons melted shortening. Spread in 8-inch square pan. Combine ¼ cup brown sugar, 1 teaspoon cinnamon, 1 tablespoon each flour and melted butter, ⅓ cup chopped nutmeats; sprinkle on batter; bake at 375° for 25 to 30 minutes.

CREPES SUZETTES: Combine 3 beaten eggs, ½ cup milk. Add ½ cup pancake mix, 1 teaspoon grated lemon peel. Heat 1 teaspoon butter in small frying pan. Coat bottom of pan with a thin layer of batter. When underside is browned, turn. Cook each crepe in this way. Roll up; serve with fruit sauce.

DOUGHNUTS: Mix 3 cups buckwheat pancake mix, ⅔ cup sugar, 1½ teaspoons cinnamon, ½ teaspoon nutmeg. Combine 2 beaten eggs, ¾ cup milk; add. Add 2 tablespoons melted shortening. Roll ½-inch thick. Cut with doughnut cutter. Fry in vegetable oil, 2 inches deep, heated to 375°.

CORN PANCAKES: Add 1 cup drained kernel corn to package recipe for buckwheat pancake batter. Bake on hot griddle. Serve with pork sausage in a creamy pan gravy.

CHEESE PANCAKES: Add ⅔ cup grated American cheddar cheese to package recipe for pancake batter. Bake on hot griddle. Serve with hot applesauce and crisp bacon.

Four Ways With Corn Muffin Mix

RAISIN CHEESE CORN STICKS: Prepare corn muffin mix as directed on package. Stir in ½ cup each seedless raisins and grated sharp Cheddar cheese. Spoon into well-greased corn-stick pans, filling two-thirds full. Bake as directed on package. Serve hot. *Makes about 14 sticks.*

CORN DIXIES: Spoon batter into well-greased tart shell pans or large muffin pans, filling two-thirds full. Bake as directed for 15 minutes. Combine ½ cup peanut butter, ½ cup dairy sour cream, ¼ cup brown sugar and ½ cup chopped peanuts. Spread thickly on partly baked Dixies. Bake 10 minutes longer. *Makes 8 to 10.*

BACON SQUARES: Stir ½ to 1 cup drained whole kernel corn into batter. Spoon into well-greased 8 or 9-inch square pan. Crumble 6 crisply cooked bacon strips; scatter on top. Bake as directed on package. *Makes 9 to 12 squares.*

APPLECORN GRIDDLE CAKES: Combine 1 package corn muffin mix, 1½ cups finely chopped apples and 2 tablespoons sugar. Add ¼ teaspoon baking soda to 1½ cups buttermilk; add with 1 beaten egg and 2 tablespoons vegetable oil to apple mixture. Let stand 10 minutes. Bake on hot griddle.
Makes about 18 griddle cakes 4 inches in diameter.

Tea Party Loaf

3 cups prepared biscuit mix	1½ cups milk
1 cup quick rolled oats (uncooked)	¼ cup vegetable oil
1 cup sugar	1 pkg. (6 oz.) semi-sweet chocolate pieces
1 egg, slightly beaten	½ cup chopped walnuts

Measure biscuit mix into bowl; stir in rolled oats and sugar. Combine egg, milk and oil; add to oat mixture; beat until smooth. Stir in chocolate pieces and nuts. Turn into greased and wax-paper lined 9 x 5 x 3-inch loaf pan. Bake at 350° for 1 hour and 15 minutes, or until cake tester inserted in center comes out clean. Cool 10 minutes before turning out of pan.

Bunker Hill Brown Bread

1½ cups sifted all-purpose flour
2 teaspoons baking soda
1½ teaspoons salt
1 cup wheat germ
1 cup graham cracker crumbs
2 eggs
⅓ cup vegetable oil
1 cup light molasses
2 cups buttermilk

Mix and sift flour, baking soda and salt. Stir in wheat germ and graham cracker crumbs. Combine eggs, oil, molasses and buttermilk. Beat to blend. Add to dry ingredients; stir until well blended. Turn into 2 well-greased and floured tall 1-lb. coffee cans; set in pan (for ease of handling); do not cover. Bake at 350° for 50 to 55 minutes or until cake tester inserted in center comes out clean. Cool in cans on rack 10 minutes. Run knife carefully around loaf to base of can to loosen. Turn out of cans.

Streamlined White Batter Bread

1 package active dry yeast
1¼ cups warm water (105° to 115°)
2 tablespoons soft shortening
2 teaspoons salt
2 tablespoons sugar
3 cups sifted all-purpose flour

Dissolve yeast in warm water. Add shortening, salt, sugar and half the flour. Beat 2 minutes, medium speed on mixer or 300 vigorous strokes by hand. Scrape sides and bottom of bowl frequently. Add remaining flour; blend with spoon until smooth. Scrape batter from sides of bowl. Cover with cloth; let rise in warm place (85°) until double (about 30 minutes). Stir down batter by beating about 25 strokes. Spread batter evenly in greased 9 x 5 x 3-inch loaf pan. Batter will be sticky. Smooth out top of loaf by flouring hand and patting into shape. Let rise in warm place (85°) until batter reaches 1-inch from top of pan (about 40 minutes). Bake at 375° for 45 to 50 minutes or until brown. To test loaf, tap the top crust; it should sound hollow. Remove from pan to rack. Brush top with melted butter. Do not place in draft.

Cranberry Wheat Germ Bread

2 cups sifted all-purpose
    flour
1 cup sugar
2 teaspoons baking powder
½ teaspoon baking soda
1½ teaspoons salt
1 cup halved raw
    cranberries

½ cup chopped pecans
½ cup wheat germ
3 tablespoons grated orange
    peel
1 egg, slightly beaten
½ cup orange juice
¼ cup warm water
2 tablespoons vegetable oil

Mix and sift flour, sugar, baking powder, baking soda and salt. Stir in cranberry halves, pecans, wheat germ and orange peel. Combine egg, orange juice, water and oil. Add to flour mixture; stir just enough to moisten ingredients. Spoon into greased loaf pan 9 x 5 x 3 inches. Bake at 350° for 50 to 60 minutes or until done. Cool in pan 5 minutes; remove from pan; finish cooling on rack.

Corn Meal Batter Bread

¾ cup boiling water
½ cup yellow corn meal
3 tablespoons soft shortening
¼ cup light molasses
2 teaspoons salt

1 package active dry yeast
¼ cup warm water (105° to
    115°)
1 egg
2¾ cups sifted all-purpose
    flour

Combine first 5 ingredients in mixing bowl; mix well. Cool to lukewarm. Dissolve yeast in warm water. Add yeast, egg and half the flour to lukewarm mixture. Beat 2 minutes with electric mixer at medium speed or 300 vigorous strokes by hand. Scrape sides and bottom of bowl frequently. Add rest of flour; mix with spoon until flour is thoroughly blended into dough. Cover; let rise in warm place (85°) until double in size (about 30 minutes). Stir hard about ½ minute. Spread batter evenly in greased loaf pan 9 x 5 x 3 inches. Flour hands and smooth top of loaf. Cover; let rise until dough reaches to 1-inch from top of pan. Sprinkle top with a little corn meal and salt. Bake at 375° for 50 minutes. Remove from pan. Brush top with soft shortening.

Whole Wheat Batter Bread

1 package active dry yeast
1¼ cups warm water (105° to 115°)
2 tablespoons honey, brown sugar or molasses
1 cup unsifted whole wheat flour
2 cups sifted all-purpose flour
2 teaspoons salt
2 tablespoons soft shortening

In mixer bowl, dissolve yeast in warm water. Add honey, one-half of each kind of flour, salt and shortening. Beat 2 minutes at medium speed on mixer or 300 vigorous strokes by hand. Scrape sides and bottom of bowl frequently. With spoon, blend in remaining flour until smooth. Cover; let rise in warm place (85°) until double (about 30 minutes). Stir down batter by beating about 25 strokes. Spread batter evenly in greased loaf pan 9 x 5 x 3 inches. Batter will be sticky. Smooth out top of loaf by flouring hand and patting into shape. Let rise in warm place (85°) until batter reaches 1-inch from top of pan (about 40 minutes). Bake at 375° for 45 to 50 minutes, or until brown. To test loaf, tap the top crust. It should sound hollow. Remove from pan immediately. Place on cooling rack or across bread pan. Brush top with melted butter or margarine. Do not place in direct draft. Cool before slicing.

Crunchy Muffin-Rolls

1 package active dry yeast
¼ cup warm water (105° to 115°)
¾ cup lukewarm milk
1 egg, beaten
1 teaspoon salt
1 tablespoon sugar
½ cup melted butter or margarine
2 cups all-purpose flour
½ cup wheat germ

Dissolve yeast in warm water; add to lukewarm milk; stir in next 4 ingredients. Mix in flour and wheat germ; stir smooth. Turn batter into greased bowl; brush with additional butter; cover; let rise until almost doubled. Stir down. Spread additional wheat germ in shallow bowl. Drop spoonfuls of batter into wheat germ; lift into well-greased muffin cups. Let rise about 40 minutes, or until doubled and very light. Bake at 400° about 15 minutes. *Makes 12 rolls.*

Oatmeal Batter Bread

1 package active dry yeast
1¼ cups warm water (105° to 115°)
3 tablespoons sugar
1½ teaspoons salt
2 tablespoons soft shortening

2½ cups sifted all-purpose flour
1 cup rolled oats, quick or old fashioned, uncooked
½ cup golden seedless raisins

Dissolve yeast in warm water, in mixing bowl. Add sugar, salt and shortening; stir. Add 1 cup flour and oats. Beat 2 minutes with electric mixer at medium speed or 300 vigorous strokes by hand. Stir in remaining flour and raisins. Cover; let rise in warm place (85°) until double in size. Stir hard about ½ minute. Spread batter in greased loaf pan 9 x 5 x 3 inches. Cover; let rise until batter is 1-inch from top of pan. Bake at 375° for 45 minutes. Remove from pan. Brush with soft shortening.

French Bread

2½ cups warm water (105° to 115°)
1 tablespoon sugar
1 tablespoon salt
1 package active dry yeast
8½ cups sifted all-purpose flour

2 tablespoons soft shortening
Corn meal
½ cup water
½ teaspoon salt
1½ teaspoons cornstarch
Sesame seeds

Combine first 4 ingredients; stir to dissolve yeast; let stand 5 minutes. Stir in flour and shortening; then work flour in with hands. Knead until smooth and elastic. Cover; let rise in warm place (85°) until doubled. Shape into 3 balls. Let rest 15 minutes. Shape each ball into a roll 15 inches long, tapered at each end. Place on baking sheet liberally sprinkled with cornmeal. Cover with towel; let rise until light. Meanwhile combine water, remaining salt and cornstarch. Cook and stir until thickened and clear. Brush over loaves; sprinkle tops with sesame seeds. Make several diagonal gashes ½-inch deep in top of each loaf. Heat oven to 450°. Place a large pan of hot water on lower shelf. Place bread on upper shelf; bake 10 minutes; reduce heat to 350°; bake 50 to 60 minutes longer.

Makes 3 loaves.

Orange-Carrot Bread

2 packages active dry yeast
1 cup warm water (105° to 115°)
2 tablespoons sugar
2 teaspoons salt
½ teaspoon cinnamon
¼ teaspoon nutmeg
¼ teaspoon allspice
1 egg, beaten

3 tablespoons butter or margarine
⅔ cup lukewarm orange juice
2 tablespoons grated orange peel
6 to 6½ cups sifted all-purpose flour, divided
1 cup seedless raisins

1½ cups grated raw carrots, at room temperature

Sprinkle yeast on warm water; stir until dissolved. Add sugar, salt, spices, egg, butter, orange juice and peel. Stir in 3 cups of the flour. Beat until smooth. Add raisins and carrots; blend well. Gradually add enough remaining flour to make a soft dough. Turn out on lightly-floured board; knead until smooth, about 5 to 8 minutes. Place in greased bowl, turning to grease top. Cover; let rise in warm place (85°), free from draft, until double in bulk (about 1 hour). Divide in half; shape each half into a loaf. Place each loaf in greased 9 x 5 x 3-inch loaf pan. Cover; let rise in warm place until doubled (about 1 hour). Bake at 400° about 35 to 40 minutes, or until done. Remove from pan; cool on rack.   *Makes 2 loaves.*

Challah

1 package active dry yeast
¼ cup warm water (105° to 115°)
2 teaspoons sugar
4½ cups sifted all-purpose flour

2 teaspoons salt
⅛ teaspoon saffron (optional)
2 eggs
2 tablespoons vegetable oil
1 cup warm water
1 egg yolk, slightly beaten

Sprinkle yeast on ¼ cup warm water; stir to dissolve; add sugar; mix well; let stand 5 minutes. Sift flour with salt and saffron. Make a "well" in center; drop in 2 eggs, oil, 1 cup warm water and yeast mixture; work into the flour. Knead on floured surface until smooth and elastic. Shape into a ball; place in greased bowl; turn over to bring greased surface to top. Cover; set in warm place (85°), free from drafts; let rise 1 hour. Punch down; cover; let rise until double in size. Divide dough into 3 equal portions. With floured hands, roll each portion in strips of equal length. Braid strips together; seal ends. Place in bread pan. Cover; let rise again until double in size. Brush with egg yolk. Bake at 350° about 50 minutes or until deep golden brown.

V. Let's Cook Out of Doors

Everyone loves a cookout. And nearly every home is equipped with a barbecue grill—from a small, portable affair for a pocket-handkerchief backyard to an imposing fieldstone structure on the grounds of a larger home! National Parks, many public beaches and lakeside resorts, all provide barbecue pits for families and groups that bring their own food for a cookout.

Picnic baskets are still packed with ready-to-eat cold foods and vacuum jugs to hold hot soup and/or coffee. You will find a complete menu for a cookout-picnic among the barbecue recipes that follow.

A word or two of caution. Foods made with eggs and milk (custards, cream fillings, mayonnaise, etc.) should be kept chilled until served. Portable ice chests make this easy.

Don't forget to take along small but necessary items such as salt, pepper, matches and fresh water for drinking, paper napkins, little dampened pads that are so refreshing for a quick clean-up. It's a good idea to make a list, tape it to a basket lid and check each item.

Be sure all fires are *completely* extinguished before you leave. And be careful all day with cigarettes, cigars, pipe ashes and matches.

Spicy Barbecued Spareribs

2 packages instant meat
    marinade
1½ cups apple cider
½ teaspoon cinnamon

¼ teaspoon each cloves and
    nutmeg
5 lbs. meaty spareribs, cut in
    serving portions

Thoroughly blend instant meat marinade with cider and spices in shallow pan. Place ribs in marinade; pierce all surfaces thoroughly with fork. Marinate 15 minutes, turning several times. Remove from marinade; drain. Pour remaining marinade into small saucepan; keep handy for basting. Place ribs on grill set 6 inches above glowing coals; barbecue total of 1 to 1½ hours (until done) turning often and brushing frequently with marinade during last 30 minutes. (Serve any remaining marinade with ribs.) *Makes 8 servings.*

Barbecue Banquet

GOLDEN BARBECUED CHICKEN: Buy broiler-fryer chickens, quartered. Brush with melted butter or margarine; brown on both sides over charcoal; place in foil pan. Grill 45 minutes, basting often with Heavenly Barbecue Sauce (about ¾ cup for 2 chickens).

HEAVENLY BARBECUE SAUCE: Pour 1½ cups molasses into large mixing bowl; gradually blend in 1 cup prepared yellow mustard. Stir in ⅓ cup Worcestershire sauce, 1½ cups vinegar, 2 teaspoons hot pepper sauce, ¼ teaspoon each marjoram and oregano. Store in tightly-covered jar in refrigerator. (It keeps.)
Makes about 1 quart.

CHILI CORN: Husk corn; spread ears with softened butter or margarine; sprinkle with salt and chili powder; double-wrap in foil; place on coals; roast 15 minutes, turning 2 or 3 times.

LUSCIOUS POTATOES: Scrub baking potatoes; rub with soft butter or margarine; double-wrap in foil; place on coals; roast 1 hour, turning several times. Break open; top with sour cream and cut chives.

SAVORY ZUCCHINI: Slice zucchini squash ½-inch thick. Combine 1 can (8 oz.) tomato sauce and 1 tablespoon instant minced onion. Place enough squash for each serving in double square of foil; top with 2 or 3 tablespoons tomato sauce, 1 teaspoon butter or margarine, salt and pepper. Gather up foil; twist top. Grill 25 minutes.

ONION BREAD CUTS: Melt ½ cup butter or margarine; add 1 tablespoon instant minced onion; let stand over low heat 10 minutes. Cut French bread loaf lengthwise, then crosswise. Brush all cut surfaces with onion-butter; wrap in foil; set on grill where heat is not too intense.

DESSERT: Thick slices of cold watermelon.

Easy Picnic

COLD BROILED CHICKEN: Have broiler-fryer chicken quartered. Brush with melted butter or margarine. Broil skin-side down, surface 3 to 4 inches below source of heat for 15 minutes; turn. Brush with butter again; broil 15 minutes longer. Chill. Sprinkle with salt and pepper; dot with butter or margarine. Wrap in aluminum foil.

CORN ON THE COB: Brush each ear of corn with melted butter or margarine; sprinkle with salt and pepper. Wrap in aluminum foil; twist ends.

RELISHES: Prepare celery, carrot sticks, radish roses. Pack with ice in covered plastic container.

FRENCH BREAD: Cut loaves almost through in 1-inch slices. Spread cut surfaces with relish sandwich spread. Wrap each loaf in aluminum foil.

FINAL COOKING: Place foil-wrapped chicken and corn on grate over glowing coals; cook 15 to 20 minutes, turning once. Place wrapped bread on grate for last 10 minutes, turning once. The ice-packed relishes will be brittle crisp; just pour off water and serve them from the container.

Buckaroo Short Ribs

2 packages instant meat
    marinade
⅔ cup tomato puree
⅔ cup red wine
2 tablespoons vinegar
2 garlic cloves, minced
2 tablespoons brown sugar

2 tablespoons prepared
    mustard
5 pounds lean, meaty, beef
    short ribs
Hickory chips
Dried rosemary leaves

Combine instant meat marinade, tomato puree, wine, vinegar, garlic, brown sugar and mustard in a shallow pan. Blend thoroughly. Pierce all surfaces of ribs deeply and thoroughly with fork, and place the ribs in the marinade. Marinate 15 minutes, turning several times. Remove meat from marinade, drain. Reserve remaining marinade for basting. Toss hickory chips and a generous pinch of rosemary on barbecue coals. Place the ribs on the grill about four or five inches from the hot coals. (Coals are ready when gray and shot with a ruddy glow.) Barbecue ribs a total of 35 to 40 minutes, turning and basting frequently with marinade. *Makes 6 servings.*

Caucasian Shashlik

2 lbs. boned lamb shoulder
2 lemons, juice
½ cup finely chopped parsley

1 teaspoon dried dillweed
1 garlic clove, slashed
Salt and pepper

Cut lamb in 1½-inch cubes; put in deep bowl. Combine remaining ingredients; pour over lamb. Chill several hours. Drain lamb. Run skewers through lamb cubes; cook over charcoal, turning often to cook evenly, about 20 minutes, or to desired degree of doneness. *Makes 4 servings.*

Chuck Wagon Beans

½ lb. Canadian bacon
½ cup diced onion
1 garlic clove, slashed
¼ teaspoon salt

4 cans (1 lb. each) red kidney beans
1 teaspoon dry mustard
½ cup light molasses

Fry Canadian bacon in skillet over outdoor grill until brown and slightly crisp. Add onion and garlic; cook until just tender, about 5 minutes. Remove garlic. Turn into deep casserole. Stir in remaining ingredients. Cover; cook over low heat at back of grill about 30 minutes. Remove cover; cook 15 minutes longer, stirring often. *Makes 6 to 8 servings.*

Savory Italian Bread

1 round loaf Italian bread
½ cup mayonnaise
¼ teaspoon garlic powder
⅓ cup minced parsley

2 tablespoons prepared mustard
½ teaspoon herb seasoning
Dash cayenne pepper

Slash bread into 8 wedges, almost to bottom crust. Combine remaining ingredients; mix well. Spread cut surface of bread with mayonnaise mixture. Wrap in heavy duty aluminum foil. Heat on grill 12 to 15 minutes. *Makes 8 servings.*

Poppyseed Loaf

Cut a small loaf of unsliced white bread in half lengthwise, almost through to bottom, then crosswise in eighths. Place on a double-thickness of heavy-duty aluminum foil. Brush all cut surfaces and outside of the loaf with melted butter or margarine. Sprinkle with poppyseeds. Wrap securely in foil; place on grill for 10 to 12 minutes.

Corn Chunks

Select tender, young ears of corn. Break each ear into 3 or 4 chunks. Roll in melted butter or margarine; sprinkle with salt and coarse black pepper. Wrap individual portions securely in double thickness of heavy aluminum foil. Grill directly on hot coals 10 to 12 minutes, turning once. Keep hot on grill. Use metal meat skewers for holders.

Zucchini Creole

6 small zucchini
3 medium tomatoes
1 teaspoon salt
¼ teaspoon coarse black pepper
½ teaspoon sugar
2 tablespoons butter or margarine

Slice zucchini crosswise in ¼-inch slices. Cube tomatoes and add to zucchini with salt, pepper and sugar. Mix well. Divide into 4 portions on 4 large squares of double heavy-duty aluminum foil. Place ½ tablespoon butter on each portion. Wrap foil securely around food. Grill over hot coals 20 to 25 minutes, turning once.

Foiled Sautéed Bananas

4 firm, green-tipped bananas
½ cup lemon juice
¼ cup melted butter or margarine
½ cup packaged seasoned bread crumb mix

Dip bananas in lemon juice; roll in melted butter, then in seasoned bread crumbs. Wrap in heavy foil; grill 10 minutes over hot coals. *Makes 4 servings.*

Regional Barbecue Sauces for Chicken

NORTH:

½ cup molasses
½ cup prepared mustard
½ cup tarragon vinegar

2 tablespoons Worcestershire
  sauce
1 teaspoon dried tarragon

Combine all ingredients; beat with rotary beater. Allow ¼ cup
for 2 broiler-fryer chicken halves.

Makes approximately 1½ cups.

EAST:

⅔ cup vegetable oil
1 cup lemon juice
½ teaspoon celery seed

2 tablespoons salt
¼ teaspoon cayenne
2 tablespoons minced onion

¼ teaspoon thyme

Combine as above.

Makes 1¾ cups.

SOUTH:

¼ cup melted butter
2 tablespoons sugar
¼ teaspoon hot pepper sauce
½ teaspoon dry mustard
½ cup vegetable oil

¼ cup catchup
1 tablespoon Worcestershire
  sauce
1 medium onion, chopped
  fine
2 tablespoons vinegar

Combine as above.

Makes approximately 1½ cups.

WEST:

¼ cup vegetable oil
½ cup lemon juice
1 garlic clove, minced
1 medium onion, chopped

2 tablespoons soy sauce
¼ teaspoon pepper
1 teaspoon each thyme, marjoram and rosemary

Combine as above.

Makes approximately 1 cup.

VI. Sandwiches

There are so many occasions when sandwiches are the ideal choice for a luncheon or supper main dish. A beautiful, frosted sandwich loaf is perfect fare for an all-girl luncheon; soup and grilled sandwiches, with a simple dessert, is a Sunday night supper menu that can be repeated often: Little Heroes or Hootenanny Sandwiches are hearty enough to satisfy a crowd of teen-age boys; Toasted Bacon Rolls are recommended for a lazy holiday brunch; other uses and other occasions will suggest themselves as you read the recipes that follow.

Chicken Curry Sandwich Spread

1½ cups chopped cooked or canned chicken
2 tablespoons finely chopped onion
½ cup chopped sweet mixed pickles
1 teaspoon curry powder
¼ cup mayonnaise
Salt and pepper to taste

Combine chicken, onion and pickles; mix lightly. Blend curry powder and mayonnaise, add to chicken mixture, mix thoroughly. Season to taste with salt and pepper. *Makes about 2 cups.*

Deviled Skillet Sandwiches

1 large can (4½ oz.) deviled ham
½ cup finely diced celery
½ cup well-drained sweet pickle relish

¼ cup mayonnaise
12 slices white bread
2 eggs
1 cup milk
Butter or margarine

Mix together deviled ham, celery, relish and mayonnaise. Spread on bread to make six closed sandwiches. Beat eggs slightly with milk. Dip each sandwich in egg mixture; brown on both sides in butter or margarine. Serve at once.

Mod Sandwich Loaf

Trim crust from one sandwich loaf of unsliced white bread. Cut loaf lengthwise into fourths. Cover with damp towel while preparing spreads. To assemble, spread each filling over a slice of bread and stack the slices, topping the stack with fourth slice. Soften 12 ounces cream cheese with cream to spreading consistency. Spread over sides and top of loaf. Garnish in a "mod" design with sliced stuffed olives, pitted ripe olives and strips of green pepper. Chill before serving.

KING CRAB SPREAD:

1 can (7½ oz.) Alaska king crab or ½ lb. frozen Alaska king crab

4 ozs. cream cheese
½ teaspoon celery salt

Drain and chop crab. Blend with cream cheese and celery salt. Chill.

EGG SALAD SPREAD:

4 hard-cooked eggs
¼ cup mayonnaise
1 tablespoon prepared mustard

¼ teaspoon salt
1 tablespoon snipped parsley

Sieve or chop eggs. Blend well with remaining ingredients. Chill.

CHEESE OLIVE SPREAD:

1 jar (5 oz.) sharp cheddar cheese spread	¼ cup chopped ripe olives
	¼ cup diced pimiento

Combine all ingredients; blend well. Chill.

Grilled Sandwiches

Spread 6 slices bread generously with peanut butter. Crumble crisp bacon over peanut butter; top with 6 slices of bread. Brush sandwiches on both sides with melted butter or margarine. Grill until golden brown on electric table grill or hot griddle. (Crunch-style peanut butter may be used if preferred.)

Makes 6 sandwiches.

Hep'burgers

1 lb. lean beef, ground	4 hamburger buns
1 teaspoon Ac'cent	4 tablespoons peanut butter
¾ teaspoon salt	4 slices cooked crisp bacon,
¼ teaspoon pepper	crumbled
4 pineapple slices	

Break up beef with fork in mixing bowl. Sprinkle Ac'cent, salt and pepper over entire surface of meat. Toss gently with fork to distribute seasonings. Shape into 4 patties. Pan-broil or grill to desired doneness. Spread half the bun with peanut butter; top with bacon, hamburger, pineapple slice. Cover with other half bun. Repeat for each serving. *Makes 4 servings.*

VARIATIONS:

1. Substitute deviled ham for peanut butter, onion slice for pineapple and pickle relish for bacon.
2. Substitute cheese spread for peanut butter, tomato slice for pineapple and stuffed olive for bacon.

Hootenanny Sandwiches

1 jar (12 oz.) peanut butter
½ lb. cream cheese
1 large can (4½ oz.) deviled ham
½ cup well-drained sweet pickle relish
Sliced whole wheat and white bread

Combine first 4 ingredients; beat until well blended. Spread between bread slices. Makes enough filling for 15 sandwiches.

KITCHEN HINT: Sandwiches can be made ahead of time, wrapped, frozen. They defrost rapidly.

Little Heroes

18 club rolls
Mustard
1 lb. thinly sliced Canadian-style bacon
3 packages (½ lb. each) sliced process American cheese
2 cans (1 lb. each) kidney beans
1 large dill pickle, chopped
1 or 2 Spanish or Bermuda onions, thinly sliced
Melted butter or margarine

Cut each roll into 3 lengthwise slices. Spread bottom slice with mustard, top with 1 slice Canadian-style bacon, 1 slice cheese. (Cut bacon and cheese slices in half to fit roll). Add middle slice of roll. Top with slightly mashed beans and sprinkle with chopped pickle; add sliced onion. Add top slice of roll. Brush with melted butter or margarine. Place in 425° oven for a few minutes, until cheese begins to melt. *Makes 18 servings.*

Salad-Sandwich Loaf

Remove crusts from unsliced loaf. Cut lengthwise into 5 slices. Put together with following fillings. Frost as directed. Chill. Slice crosswise to serve.

1st LAYER: Combine ½ cup flaked salmon, 2 tablespoons each drained pickle relish, minced celery, mayonnaise.

2nd LAYER: Combine ½ cup creamed cottage cheese, 1 tablespoon cut chives, 2 tablespoons each chopped stuffed olives and cream.

3rd LAYER: Combine 2 hard-cooked eggs, chopped, with ¼ cup each minced green pepper and chili sauce.

4th LAYER: Combine 1 large can (4½ oz.) deviled ham, 2 tablespoons mayonnaise, ¼ cup minced cucumber and 1 tablespoon minced pimiento.

FROSTING: Mash ¾ lb. (12 oz.) cream cheese; add 1½ tablespoons each mayonnaise and cream. Whip until fluffy. Spread on top and sides of loaf. Garnish with "flowers" made of black olive petals, stuffed olive centers and green pepper stems.

Toasted Bacon Rolls

Split frankfurter rolls. Toast. Spread 1 side with butter or margarine, the other side with marmalade. Fill with two slices of crisp bacon. Keep hot at 250° until ready to serve.

VII. Happy Endings (Desserts)

CAKES

It used to be said that if a cook had a knack for cakes, her pies left something to be desired, and vice versa. Thank goodness that's no longer true. In the wonderful world of mixes, never-fail cakes, quick-as-a-wink frostings and light, flaky pastry are every women's prerogatives.

All that is necessary is to add a touch of one's own to make a cake that is different and distinctively your own.

Just follow package directions exactly, use a pan of the size specified, set the oven for correct temperature and the timer for the length of time required.

The venturesome, who want to try their hand at making a cake from scratch, will find recipes of this type, too.

Viennese Torte

1 package chocolate cake
    mix
¾ cup apricot preserves
3 tablespoons boiling water
1 pkg. (6 oz.) semi-sweet
    chocolate pieces

1 tablespoon shortening
3 tablespoons light corn
    syrup
2 tablespoons milk
½ cup chopped almonds or
    pistachio nuts

Prepare and bake cake mix as directed on package for two 8-inch layers. Cool. Cut each layer in half crosswise to make 4 thin layers. Break up preserves with fork; add water; beat smooth. Spread between layers, on sides and on top. Chill thoroughly. Melt chocolate and shortening over hot (not boiling) water. Remove from heat; blend in corn syrup and milk. Pour warm frosting over chilled torte; smooth with spatula. Garnish with chopped nuts.

Chocolate-Cherry Kuchen

¾ cup butter or margarine
3 squares (1 oz. each) un-
    sweetened chocolate
1½ cups sugar
3 eggs, beaten
1½ cups sifted cake flour

½ teaspoon baking powder
½ teaspoon salt
1 can (1 lb.) pitted sour red
    cherries
1½ teaspoons vanilla
1 cup whipping cream

Melt butter or margarine and chocolate together over hot water. Add sugar to beaten eggs gradually while beating. Add chocolate mixture to egg mixture; beat hard 1 minute. Mix and sift flour, baking powder and salt. Drain cherries thoroughly; add to flour mixture, stir into chocolate-egg mixture. Stir in vanilla. Divide batter evenly between 2 greased and floured 9-inch layer cake pans. Bake at 350° for 35 to 40 minutes. Cool. Whip cream; spread between layers and on top of cake. Chill.

Picnic Cake

1 package cake mix (any fa-
    vorite flavor)
⅓ cup butter or margarine
⅔ cup firmly packed light
    brown sugar

¼ cup evaporated milk
1½ cups flaked coconut
1 teaspoon vanilla

Prepare cake mix as directed on package; turn into well-greased and floured oblong pan 9 x 13 x 2 inches. Bake as directed. Cool slightly in pan. Cream butter or margarine until fluffy. Add sugar gradually, while creaming. Add remaining ingredients; mix well. Spread over top of cake. Broil, with surface of frosting about 4 inches below source of heat, until coconut is delicately browned. Cool in pan; cut in squares to serve.

Chocolate Cake Log

½ teaspoon salt
4 eggs
¾ cup sugar

2 squares (1 oz. each)
  unsweetened chocolate,
  melted
1 teaspoon vanilla
¾ cup pancake mix

Add salt to eggs; beat until thick and lemon-colored. Add sugar, a little at a time, beating well after each addition. Add melted chocolate, vanilla and pancake mix; stir lightly until batter is smooth. Spread batter evenly in greased, waxed-paper-lined jelly-roll pan, 10 x 15 x 1 inches. Bake at 400° for 10 to 12 minutes. While cake is baking, sprinkle a dry towel with confectioners' (powdered) sugar. When cake is done, loosen edges at once; turn out on towel. Peel waxed paper carefully from cake. Roll cake quickly in towel. Let stand 20 minutes; unroll. Spread with softened ice cream or whipped cream or whipped topping. Roll up quickly. Wrap cake in aluminum foil; chill. If ice cream is used as filling; place in freezer for several hours. (May be made a day or two in advance.) Frost with Mocha Butter Frosting (below); put through a pastry tube to resemble bark. Make snow drifts with confectioners' sugar. *Makes 8 to 10 servings.*

MOCHA BUTTER FROSTING:

½ lb. unsalted butter
½ cup sugar
 1 teaspoon Dutch process
   cocoa

1 tablespoon instant coffee
  powder

Cream butter to consistency of mayonnaise. Combine sugar, cocoa, and coffee; sift through fine sieve. Add sugar mixture, 1 tablespoon at a time, to butter; be sure to cream thoroughly after each addition is made.

Refrigerator Fruit Cake

1½ cups seedless raisins
1 cup pitted prunes
1 cup sliced pitted dates
1½ cups mixed, diced candied
    fruits and peels
½ cup butter or margarine
½ cup confectioners' sugar
¼ cup light corn syrup

½ cup orange marmalade
1 teaspoon cinnamon
¼ teaspoon cloves
½ teaspoon salt
½ cup chopped walnuts
5 cups fine graham cracker
    crumbs

Rinse and drain raisins and prunes. Pour boiling water over prunes, let stand 5 minutes; drain; cool; slice. Combine all fruits and peels. Cream butter and sugar together. Blend in syrup, marmalade, spices and salt. Mix lightly with fruits. Let stand 2 hours or longer. Blend in walnuts and crumbs. Pack into loaf pan 9 x 5 x 3 inches which has been lined with waxed paper. Chill 48 hours, or longer.

Chocolate Cherry Fruit Cake

3 eggs, well beaten
1 cup sugar
1½ cups sifted all-purpose
    flour
1½ teaspoons baking powder
¼ teaspoon salt

1 pkg. (6 oz.) semi-sweet
    chocolate pieces, divided
2 cups coarsely chopped
    pecans or walnuts
1 cup coarsely cut dates
1 cup halved candied cherries

Beat eggs and sugar together. Sift dry ingredients. Add ¾ cup chocolate pieces, nuts, dates and cherries to flour; fold in egg-sugar mixture. Spoon into oiled, waxed-paper-lined loaf pan, 9 x 5 x 3 inches. Scatter remaining chocolate pieces on top. Bake at 325° for 1¼ hours or until crusty brown; remove; cool on rack.

Madcap Cake

1½ cups sifted all-purpose
    flour
3 tablespoons breakfast
    cocoa (not instant)
1 cup sugar

1 teaspoon baking soda
½ teaspoon salt
1 teaspoon vinegar
1 teaspoon vanilla
5 tablespoons vegetable oil

1 cup water

Sift first 5 ingredients into greased 8-inch square cake pan. Make 3 depressions in dry ingredients. Pour vinegar into one, vanilla into another, vegetable oil into the third. Pour water over all. Mix well, until smooth. Bake at 350° for 35 minutes. When cool, frost as desired or serve with ice cream and chocolate sauce.

Makes 9 servings.

Saucy Surprise Cake

1½ cups sifted all-purpose
    flour
2 teaspoons baking powder
1 teaspoon salt
½ cup butter or margarine
    divided

⅔ cup sugar
1 cup milk
½ cup seedless raisins
1 lemon, grated peel and
    juice
½ cup light molasses

1¼ cups water

Mix and sift flour, baking powder and salt. Cream 4 tablespoons butter or margarine. Gradually add sugar; cream until light and fluffy. Add milk alternately with flour mixture; beating smooth after each addition. Stir in raisins and lemon peel. Spoon into well greased 8-inch square cake pan. Combine lemon juice, remaining butter, molasses and water in saucepan. Bring to boil. Remove from heat; pour gently and evenly over batter. Bake at 350° for 45 to 50 minutes. Serve warm. *Makes 9 servings.*

Sherry Cinnamon Coffee Squares

1 package yellow cake mix
1½ teaspoons cinnamon,
    divided
⅓ cup sherry

Milk or water
½ cup firmly packed brown
    sugar
½ cup chopped walnuts

Prepare cake batter according to directions on package of cake mix, adding 1 teaspoon cinnamon to the mix and substituting ⅓ cup sherry for ⅓ cup of the required milk or water. Pour batter into greased and floured 9 x 13 x 2-inch baking pan. Mix brown sugar, walnuts and remaining ½ teaspoon cinnamon; sprinkle over top of batter. Bake as directed on package. Cut in squares; serve warm.

COOKIES

In these lucky days, there is no need for any home to be without a supply of cookies. (And how welcome they are when your children bring friends home from school, when neighbors drop in for a chat, when unexpected guests stop by for an evening!) There are packaged cookies, all ready to serve, in keep-crisp boxes or bags, rolls of refrigerated cookie dough, ready to slice and bake or packaged cookie mixes for brownies, bar cookies, drop or roll cookies.

However, there are times when it is fun to make a batch of cookies from beginning to end, and there are still some types that are not to be found in the market place. The following recipes are favorites. Enjoy them!

Angel Whispers

1 cup butter or margarine	2 cups sifted all-purpose
½ cup sifted confectioners'	flour
(powdered) sugar	¼ teaspoon salt
1 teaspoon lemon extract	Lemon Filling (below)

Cream butter to consistency of mayonnaise. Add sugar gradually while continuing to cream. Add remaining ingredients; blend well. Chill. Measure level teaspoon of dough; round into ball; flatten slightly. Place about 1 inch apart on ungreased baking sheet. Bake at 400° for 8 to 10 minutes or until edges are lightly browned. Put together with Lemon Filling.

Makes about 5 dozen double cookies.

LEMON FILLING:

1 egg, slightly beaten
  Grated peel of 1 lemon
⅔ cup sugar

2 tablespoons lemon juice
1½ tablespoons soft butter or
  margarine

Blend all ingredients in top of double boiler. Cook over hot water, stirring constantly, until thick. Chill until firm.

Breakfast Cookies

1¼ cups unsifted all-purpose
  flour
⅔ cup sugar
½ cup grape-nuts cereal
1 teaspoon baking powder
½ pound bacon, cooked and
  crumbled

½ cup soft-type margarine
1 egg
2 tablespoons frozen orange
  juice concentrate,
  thawed, undiluted
1 tablespoon grated orange
  peel

Measure flour, sugar, grape-nuts and baking powder into mixing bowl; mix well. Add bacon, margarine, egg, orange juice concentrate and peel. Mix until well blended. Drop by level tablespoons 2 inches apart on ungreased baking sheet. Bake at 350° for 10 to 12 minutes or until edges of cookies are lightly browned but cookies are still soft. Remove from baking sheet immediately. *Makes 2½ dozen cookies.*

Brownie-Peanut Cookies

1 egg
½ cup chopped peanuts

3 tablespoons peanut butter
1 package brownie mix

Add egg, chopped peanuts and peanut butter to mix. Blend with hands, adding a few drops of water if necessary. Press and shape into long roll, about 2 inches in diameter. Slice ⅛-inch thick. Bake at 375° for about 5 minutes on ungreased baking sheets. Cool slightly before removing from baking sheets.

Makes about 4 dozen.

Butter-Crisps

1 lb. soft butter or margarine
2 cups flour

1 cup confectioners'
  (powdered) sugar
1 cup cornstarch*

Cream butter. Add flour, sugar and cornstarch slowly while continuing to cream. Divide into 4 portions. Wrap each portion in foil. Chill thoroughly. Shape into 1-inch balls, working quickly with 1 portion of dough at a time, keeping other portions in the refrigerator. Place balls 2 inches apart on ungreased cookie sheet. Flatten with floured tines of fork. Bake at 325° for 18 to 20 minutes, or until lightly browned. *Makes about 7 dozen.*

*(This amount of cornstarch is correct!)

Cherry Chip Cookies

½ cup butter or margarine,
  softened
1 package (3 oz.) cream
  cheese, softened
1 egg
½ cup finely chopped candied
  cherries
1 teaspoon almond extract

½ cup sugar
1¼ cups sifted all-purpose
  flour
½ teaspoon salt
½ teaspoon baking powder
¾ cup rolled oats, quick
  or old fashioned,
  uncooked

Beat butter and cream cheese together. Stir in egg, cherries and almond extract. Mix and sift sugar, flour, salt and baking powder. Add to butter mixture; beat well. Stir in oats; blend thoroughly. Chill; shape mixture into small balls about ¾ inch in diameter. Place on greased cookie sheets; flatten with bottom of glass dipped in flour. If desired, press a slice of candied cherry on top of each cookie. Bake at 375° for 10 to 12 minutes.
Makes about 4 dozen cookies.

Cherub Coins

¾ cup butter or margarine
1½ cups firmly packed light
    brown sugar
1 egg, unbeaten

2 cups sifted cake flour
⅛ teaspoon baking soda
½ teaspoon salt
¼ cup finely chopped pecans

Cream butter or margarine and sugar; add egg; mix well. Mix
and sift flour, baking soda and salt; add gradually; mix well
after each addition. Stir in chopped pecans. Chill overnight.
Shape into tiny balls ½ inch in diameter. Place on greased cookie
sheets; flatten slightly with thumb. Bake on greased cookie
sheets at 375° for 8 to 10 minutes. Let stand a few minutes
before removing from cookie sheets.

Makes about 10 dozen.

Chocolate Walnut Wafers

2 squares (1 oz. each)
    unsweetened chocolate
1 cup chopped walnuts

1 can (15 oz.) sweetened con-
    densed milk

Melt chocolate over hot water. Add sweetened condensed milk;
stir until well blended. Add walnuts. Drop mixture by teaspoons
on greased baking sheet. Bake at 350° for 12 to 15 minutes.
Remove from pan at once. Cool on wire cake rack.

Makes about 36 cookies.

Johnny Appleseed's Filled Cookies

½ cup soft shortening
1 cup sugar
2 eggs
2 tablespoons cream
1 teaspoon vanilla

2½ cups sifted all-purpose
    flour
¼ teaspoon baking soda
½ teaspoon salt
    Thick apple butter

Mix shortening, sugar and eggs thoroughly. Stir in cream and vanilla. Stir flour, baking soda and salt together until thoroughly blended. Stir into egg mixture. Chill at least 1 hour. Heat oven to 400°. Roll dough about ⅛-inch thick on lightly floured pastry cloth or board. Cut rounds with floured cookie cutter 2½ inches in diameter. Place half the rounds on lightly-greased baking sheet. Top each with rounded teaspoon of thick apple butter. Make slits in remaining rounds; place these over filled rounds. Press edges together with tines of fork. Bake 8 to 10 minutes. *Makes about 2 dozen cookies.*

Quick Chocolate Cookies

1 package (4½ oz.) instant chocolate pudding mix
1 cup biscuit mix
¼ cup shortening
1 egg
3 tablespoons milk
½ cup flaked coconut
1 tablespoon grated orange peel

Combine pudding mix and biscuit mix in bowl. Cut in shortening until mixture resembles coarse meal. Stir in egg and milk; blend well. Stir in coconut and orange peel. Form dough into 1-inch balls; place on ungreased baking sheets; flatten with tines of fork. Bake at 375° for 10 to 12 minutes. Store in a container with a tight-fitting cover. *Makes about 3 dozen cookies.*

Quick Lemon Crisps

2 cups sifted all-purpose flour
¾ teaspoon baking soda
Few grains salt
¾ cup shortening
1 cup sugar
2 packages (3¾ oz. each) instant lemon pudding mix
3 eggs, slightly beaten

Sift flour with baking soda and salt. Cream shortening. Add sugar and pudding mix; cream until light and fluffy. Add eggs; mix thoroughly. Add flour mixture; beat thoroughly until well blended. Drop from teaspoon on greased baking sheet about 2½ inches apart. Bake at 375° for 8 to 10 minutes.
Makes about 6 dozen cookies.

Soft Sugar Cookies

½ cup butter or margarine
1½ cups sugar
2 eggs
1 teaspoon vanilla
3 cups sifted all-purpose
flour

1 teaspoon salt
½ teaspoon baking powder
½ teaspoon baking soda
1 cup dairy sour cream
Cinnamon-Sugar

Cream butter to consistency of mayonnaise; add sugar gradually, while continuing to cream. Add eggs one at a time, beating well after each addition. Add vanilla. Beat until light and fluffy. Mix and sift flour, salt, baking powder and baking soda. Add to creamed mixture alternately with sour cream, beginning and ending with dry ingredients. Drop by heaping teaspoons on well-greased cookie sheets, well apart. With spatula flatten into circles about 2 inches in diameter. Sprinkle with Cinnamon-Sugar. Bake at 400° for 10 to 12 minutes.   *Makes about 30 cookies.*

CHOCOLATE SUGAR COOKIES: Add 2 squares (1 oz. each) unsweetened chocolate, melted and cooled, to creamed mixture. Continue as above.

RAISIN SUGAR COOKIES: Add 1 cup seedless raisins to creamed mixture. Continue as above.

Molasses-Chocolate Bars

1 egg, beaten
½ cup sugar
½ cup light molasses
¼ cup shortening
½ teaspoon vanilla
1 cup sifted all-purpose flour

½ teaspoon salt
¼ teaspoon baking soda
⅔ cup chopped walnuts
1 pkg. (6 oz.) semi-sweet
chocolate pieces

Combine egg, sugar, molasses, shortening and vanilla. Sift in flour, salt and baking soda. Add nuts and semi-sweet chocolate pieces. Spread in greased and lightly-floured 9-inch square pan. Bake at 350° for 45 minutes. Cut into bars 1 x 3 inches.

Makes 1½ dozen.

Peanut Marguerites

1 egg white
⅔ cup sugar
¼ teaspoon almond extract
⅛ teaspoon salt
½ cup chopped peanuts

Beat egg whites stiff; add sugar and salt while beating. Fold in peanuts and almond extract. Drop by teaspoons on greased baking sheet. Bake at 325° for 15 minutes.   *Makes 2 dozen.*

Cornflake Kisses

2 egg whites
1 cup sugar
⅛ teaspoon salt
½ teaspoon orange extract
2 cups cornflakes
1 cup flaked coconut

Beat egg whites stiff but not dry. Beat sugar into egg whites gradually. Add salt and orange extract. Fold in cornflakes and coconut. Drop by teaspoons on greased cookie sheet. Bake at 350° for 10 to 12 minutes.   *Makes 2½ dozen.*

Mincemeat Oatmeal Cookies

1¼ cups sifted all-purpose flour
¾ teaspoon baking soda
½ teaspoon salt
½ cup shortening
1 cup firmly packed brown sugar
1 egg, slightly beaten
1⅓ cups mincemeat
1½ cups quick-cooking rolled oats, uncooked

Sift together flour, baking soda and salt. Cream shortening. Gradually add sugar, beating until fluffy. Beat in egg. Stir in mincemeat. Add flour mixture in 3 parts, blending well after each addition. Stir in rolled oats. Drop by teaspoons on greased cookie sheet, about 2 inches apart. Flatten cookies slightly with back of spoon. Bake at 350° until lightly browned, about 15 minutes.
Makes about 4 dozen cookies.

There are three things that can be bothersome about making pastry: cutting in the shortening until the flour-fat mixture is exactly right; adding *just enough* water, no more, no less; and rolling out the pastry and shaping it to the pan.

If the first step bothers you, begin with pie crust mix in which flour and shortening are already combined. If the second step is troublesome, work with a mix that is completely combined and shaped into sticks—1 stick per crust. If you just can't roll out pastry, buy ready-to-bake frozen pie shells or pie crust circles!

As for fillings, try those in the recipes that follow, but don't forget the ready-to-use fillings in cans, such as apple and cherry, and ready-to-serve puddings; the mixes for cream fillings and whipped fillings—the variety is staggering!

Deep Dish Apple Crumb Pie

7 cups (about 3 lbs.) peeled, sliced apples
⅓ cup orange juice
½ cup firmly packed brown sugar
½ cup sugar
2 teaspoons grated orange peel
½ teaspoon nutmeg
½ teaspoon cinnamon
¼ teaspoon salt
¾ cup sifted all-purpose flour
½ cup butter or margarine
1 pint ice cream, any flavor

Place apples in deep pie pan; add orange juice. Mix together sugars, orange peel, nutmeg, cinnamon, salt and flour. Cut in butter or margarine. Spread evenly over apples. Bake at 350° for 1 hour. Serve warm or cold, with a topping of ice cream.

Makes 8 servings.

Creamy Pecan Pie

⅓ cup butter or margarine
¾ cup sugar
2 eggs, slightly beaten
½ cup dark corn syrup
¼ teaspoon salt

1 teaspoon vanilla
1¼ cups chopped pecans
1 cup dairy sour cream
1 unbaked 9-inch pie shell
Whole pecan meats

Cream butter and sugar until light and fluffy. Add eggs, corn syrup, salt and vanilla; mix well. Stir in chopped pecans and sour cream. Pour into pie shell. Garnish surface with whole pecan meats. Bake at 375° for 40 to 45 minutes.

Apple Pumpkin Pie

1 can (1 lb. 9 oz.) apple pie filling*
1 unbaked 10-inch pie shell**
1 tablespoon cornstarch
½ teaspoon each cinnamon, nutmeg and ginger
¼ teaspoon powdered cloves

½ teaspoon salt
1 cup sugar
1 can (1 lb.) pumpkin
2 tablespoons molasses
1½ tablespoons melted butter or margarine
1¼ cups milk
2 eggs, slightly beaten

Pour apple pie filling into unbaked pie shell. Combine cornstarch, spices, salt, sugar. Add pumpkin, molasses, melted butter or margarine; blend well. Combine milk and eggs; stir in. Pour over apple filling. (To avoid spills, add the last of the milk and egg mixture with pie on oven rack—pan will be brimful.) Bake at 425° for 40 minutes or until knife inserted in pumpkin mixture near rim comes out clean. Chill, then garnish with whipped cream.

*(Be sure to use completely prepared pie filling—not pie sliced apples which are packed in smaller cans.)

**(Use a *deep* 10-inch pie pan.)

Florida Lime Pie

1 envelope (1 tablespoon)
　unflavored gelatin
¼ cup cold water
4 eggs, separated
1 cup sugar, divided
⅓ cup lime juice

½ teaspoon salt
2 teaspoons grated lime peel
Green food coloring
1 9-inch baked pie shell or
　crumb crust

Soften gelatin in cold water. Beat egg yolks; add ½ cup sugar, lime juice, and salt. Cook over hot water, stirring constantly, until thickened. Add grated peel and gelatin; stir until gelatin is dissolved. Tint pale green with food coloring. Cool. Beat egg whites stiff but not dry; add remaining sugar slowly, beating after each addition; fold into lime mixture. Pour into pie shell; chill until firm.

Easy Lemon Chiffon Pie

1 package (3 oz.) lemon-
　flavor gelatin
¾ cup boiling water
½ cup sugar

1 lemon, juice and grated peel
1 tall can (1⅔ cups) evapo-
　rated milk, whipped
1 9-inch baked pastry shell

Dissolve gelatin in boiling water; add sugar, lemon juice and grated peel; chill until syrupy. Fold in whipped evaporated milk. Spoon into baked pastry shell. Sprinkle with toasted coconut, if desired. Chill until firm.

VARIATION: Fold in 1 cup cultivated blueberries with the whipped evaporated milk.

Golden Raisin Rhubarb Pie

Pastry for 2-crust, 9-inch
　pie
6 tablespoons flour, divided
1¼ cups sugar, divided

3 cups unpeeled rhubarb, cut
　in 1-inch pieces
1 cup golden raisins
2 tablespoons butter or
　margarine

Line 9-inch pie pan with pastry. Brush with a little melted butter or margarine; chill. Combine 2 tablespoons each of the measured flour and sugar; sprinkle over chilled pastry. Combine rhubarb and raisins; pour into pie pan. Combine remaining flour and sugar; sprinkle over rhubarb mixture. Dot with butter or margarine. Cut remaining pastry into strips for lattice topping. Bake at 450° for 15 minutes; lower heat to 350°, bake 40 to 45 minutes longer.

Quick Nesselrode Pie

1 package (3 oz.) lemon-flavor gelatin
1 cup whipping cream
½ cup broken pecan meats
½ cup chopped Maraschino cherries
1 teaspoon rum flavoring
Cereal Crumb Crust (below)

Prepare gelatin as directed on package. Chill until syrupy. Whip with rotary egg beater until light and fluffy. Whip cream; fold in with pecans, cherries and rum flavoring. Spoon lightly into crumb crust. Chill until set.

CEREAL CRUMB CRUST:

1¼ cups fine cereal flake crumbs
⅓ cup melted butter or margarine
¼ cup sugar

Combine all ingredients; mix well. Press firmly into 9-inch pie pan. Bake at 325° for 8 minutes. Cool.

MISCELLANEOUS DESSERTS

Puddings, ice cream, gelatin, fruit—plain and fancy desserts—loved by family and company.

Leaf through the pages that follow, stop now and then to

read a recipe through. Make a mental note to try this one or that one for Sunday dinner.

We just hope that no one in your family has to count calories!

Christmas Plum Pudding

1¼ cups seedless raisins
¾ cup dried currants
¾ cup finely chopped mixed candied fruits
½ cup chopped nutmeats
1 cup sifted all-purpose flour, divided
2 eggs, beaten
¾ teaspoon salt

¾ cup light molasses
¾ cup buttermilk
½ cup finely chopped suet
¼ cup fruit juice
1 cup fine dry bread crumbs
¾ teaspoon baking soda
¼ teaspoon each—cloves, allspice, cinnamon, nutmeg

Combine raisins, currants, candied fruits, nutmeats and ½ cup flour; mix well. Combine eggs, molasses, buttermilk, suet and fruit juice. Combine remaining flour, crumbs, baking soda, spices and salt; add to egg mixture. Add floured fruits and nuts; mix well. Pour into greased 1½-quart mold; cover; set on rack in deep kettle; add boiling water to about 1 inch below cover of mold. Cover. Steam 1½ to 2 hours. Serve with hard sauce.

Makes 10 to 12 servings.

Baked Pumpkin Whip
[cover illustration]

1½ cups canned pumpkin
½ cup sugar
½ teaspoon cinnamon
¼ teaspoon nutmeg

8 cooked chestnuts, ground (or save 4 halves for garnish, if desired)
4 egg whites
½ teaspoon salt
¼ teaspoon lemon juice

Combine pumpkin, sugar, cinnamon, nutmeg and ground chestnuts; set aside. Beat egg whites until foamy; add salt and lemon juice; whip until stiff. Fold into pumpkin mixture. Spoon into 4 individual baking dishes; set in pan of hot water. Bake at 300° for 40 minutes. *Makes 4 servings.*

Lemon Tapioca Parfait

¼ cup quick-cooking tapioca
¾ cup sugar
¼ teaspoon salt
2¼ cups water
¼ cup lemon juice

2 teaspoons grated lemon
   peel
½ cup whipping cream
1 cup crushed, sweetened
   red raspberries

Combine tapioca, sugar, salt and water. Let stand 5 minutes. Bring to a boil over medium heat, stirring occasionally. Remove from heat. Stir in lemon juice and peel. Cool. Whip cream; fold in. Chill. Spoon tapioca and raspberries alternately into parfait glasses, ending with raspberries. Garnish with whipped cream if desired. *Makes 6 servings.*

Bonbon Ice Cream Loaf

1 pint each of 4 different flavors ice cream and sherbet
     Colored sugar

2 quarts chocolate ice cream
½ pint whipping cream

Chill loaf pan 9 x 5 x 3 inches. With a small ice cream scoop, shape balls of ice cream and sherbet (except chocolate) and place them in freezer trays; chill until very firm. Soften chocolate ice cream; whip until fluffy. Place a layer of ice cream balls in assorted colors in bottom of chilled loaf pan. Fill spaces with whipped chocolate ice cream. Repeat until pan is filled. Freeze overnight or several hours. Invert on platter. Apply moist warm cloths to bottom and sides of pan (this takes patience) until ice cream loaf slips out. Return to freezing section until very firm again. Frost top and sides with whipped cream, putting some of it through a pastry tube for garnish. Sprinkle with colored sugar. Keep in freezing compartment until ready to serve. *Makes 12 to 16 slices.*

Lemon Ice Cream

2 eggs
½ cup sugar
½ cup light corn syrup
1 tablespoon grated lemon peel

1½ cups milk
⅔ cup whipping cream
½ cup lemon juice

Beat eggs thoroughly; add sugar gradually while beating. Add corn syrup, milk, cream, lemon juice and peel. Freeze firm. Turn out into chilled bowl. Beat with rotary beater until light. Freeze firm. *Makes 6 servings.*

Frozen Lemon Velvet

1 can (15 oz.) sweetened condensed milk
½ cup lemon juice

1 teaspoon grated lemon peel
2 eggs, separated
¼ cup sugar

Combine condensed milk, lemon juice, lemon peel and egg yolks; stir until mixture thickens. Beat egg whites until almost stiff enough to hold a peak. Add sugar gradually, beating until stiff but not dry. Slowly pour condensed milk mixture over beaten egg whites, folding in carefully. Pour mixture into freezer tray. Freeze until firm; about 2 to 3 hours. *Makes 6 servings.*

Frosty Chocolate Log

4 cups puffed rice
½ cup chopped nutmeats
28 large marshmallows
2 squares (1 oz. each) unsweetened chocolate

3 tablespoons butter or margarine
1 teaspoon vanilla
1 quart ice cream, any flavor

Heat puffed rice in shallow pan at 350° for 10 minutes. Pour into large greased bowl; stir in chopped nutmeats. Combine marshmallows, chocolate and butter in top of double boiler. Heat over boiling water until melted, stirring occasionally. Stir in vanilla. Pour marshmallow mixture over cereal and nutmeats, stirring until all kernels are evenly coated. Butter hands and, working quickly, shape mixture around well greased rolling pin. Chill until firm. Remove rolling pin, being careful not to break chocolate shell. Fill hollow center with ice cream. Freeze until firm. Let stand at room temperature a few minutes, then slice crosswise with sharp knife. *Makes 6 to 8 servings.*

Chocolate Mint Ice Cream

1 package chocolate pudding   2 cups milk
    mix (not instant)   ¼ teaspoon peppermint
¼ cup sugar   extract
       1 cup whipping cream

Combine pudding mix and sugar in saucepan. Add milk gradually, stirring constantly. Cook and stir over medium heat until mixture comes to a boil and is thickened, about 5 minutes. Remove from heat. Stir in peppermint extract. Cool slightly. Turn into freezing tray. Chill in freezer ½ hour. Remove to bowl; whip cream; fold in; return to tray. Freeze 1 hour longer; return to bowl; beat with rotary beater until smooth but not melted. Return to tray; freeze until firm, at least 3 to 4 hours.

Makes about 1 quart.

Cantaloupe a la Mode With Blueberry Sauce

½ cup sugar   1 cup cultivated blueberries
½ cup water   1 teaspoon grated lemon peel
⅛ teaspoon salt   1 tablespoon lemon juice
  1 tablespoon cornstarch   3 small cantaloupes
       1 quart vanilla ice cream

Combine sugar, water, salt and cornstarch. Cook, stirring frequently, until mixture boils and is thickened. Add blueberries; heat to boiling; simmer 5 minutes. Stir in lemon peel and juice. Let sauce cool slightly. Cut cantaloupes into halves. Scoop out seeds. Spoon vanilla ice cream into cantaloupe halves; top with warm blueberry sauce; serve immediately. *Makes 6 servings.*

Apple Charlotte

KUCHEN DOUGH:

1 cup sifted all-purpose flour
½ teaspoon baking powder
¼ teaspoon salt
2 tablespoons sugar

2½ tablespoons butter or
    margarine
2 eggs, beaten
2 tablespoons milk

Mix and sift flour, baking powder, salt and sugar. Work butter into mixture smoothly with wooden spoon. Beat in eggs. Stir in milk. Grease 8-inch spring form pan. With rubber spatula or spoon, spread dough on bottom and part way up the side of spring form pan (top edge of crust will be ragged).

APPLE FILLING:

5 cups sliced apples
½ cup golden raisins

⅔ cup sugar
1 teaspoon cinnamon
1 tablespoon grated lemon peel

Cook apple slices and raisins in enough water to cover until apples are just tender, but have not lost their shape; drain. Combine sugar, cinnamon and lemon peel; stir gently into apples and raisins. Spoon into dough-lined spring form pan. Bake at 425° for 50 to 60 minutes or until crust is deep golden brown and filling is firm. Serve hot, topped with almond-flavored and sweetened whipped cream.

Strawberry Glaze No-Bake Cheesecake

2 envelopes unflavored
    gelatin
1 cup sugar, divided
¼ teaspoon salt
2 eggs, separated
1 cup milk

1 teaspoon grated lemon peel
3 cups (24 oz.) creamed cot-
    tage cheese
1 tablespoon lemon juice
1 teaspoon vanilla
1 cup whipping cream

Line sides of 8-inch spring-form pan with waxed paper; set aside. Combine gelatin, ¾ cup sugar and salt in top of double boiler. Beat eggs yolks and milk; add to gelatin mixture. Stir over boiling water until gelatin is dissolved (about 6 minutes). Remove from heat; add lemon peel. Chill until mixture mounds slightly when dropped from a spoon. Beat cottage cheese on high speed of electric mixer 3 minutes. Stir in lemon juice and vanilla; stir into gelatin mixture. Beat egg whites until stiff, but not dry. Add remaining ¼ cup sugar gradually; beat until very stiff. Fold into gelatin mixture. Whip cream; fold in. Turn into prepared pan; chill until firm. Remove from pan. Top with Strawberry Glaze. *Makes 8 to 10 servings.*

STRAWBERRY GLAZE:

1 quart strawberries	⅔ cup sugar
¾ cup water, divided	2 tablespoons cornstarch

Wash and hull strawberries. Combine 1 cup berries with ½ cup water and sugar in saucepan. Bring to boil; lower heat; simmer 15 minutes. Blend cornstarch with remaining water. Gradually add to hot mixture, stirring constantly. Cook, stirring until thickened and clear. Remove from heat; strain through sieve. Cool. Put remaining strawberries on top of cheesecake; spoon glaze over top. Chill several hours.

Molasses Chiffon Mold

2 envelopes unflavored gelatin	½ cup molasses
	⅛ teaspoon cinnamon
1 cup cold, strong coffee, divided	½ teaspoon salt
	3 eggs, separated
⅛ teaspoon cream of tartar	3 tablespoons sugar
1 cup finely chopped walnuts	

Soften gelatin in ½ cup cold coffee. Stir cream of tartar into molasses; add cinnamon, salt and remaining coffee. Beat egg yolks until thick; add molasses mixture. Cook over hot water, stirring constantly until slightly thickened; add softened gelatin; stir until dissolved. Chill until syrupy. Beat egg whites stiff; beat sugar into egg whites, 1 tablespoon at a time; fold into gelatin mixture with chopped walnuts. Spoon into 5-cup mold; chill until set. Unmold. Garnish with whipped cream and grated chocolate, if desired. *Makes 8 servings.*

Coffee House Ginger-Date Roll

1½ cups fine gingersnap
  crumbs, divided
¾ cup finely cut dates

1 cup broken nutmeats
¼ cup strong coffee
1 lb. marshmallows, cut fine

Reserve ½ cup crumbs. Combine remaining ingredients; mix thoroughly; form into roll; coat with reserved crumbs; chill thoroughly. Slice; serve with whipped cream.   *Makes 8 servings.*

Cream Puffs

½ cup butter or margarine
1 cup boiling water

1 cup sifted all-purpose flour
4 eggs

Melt butter or margarine in boiling water in saucepan; bring to boil; lower heat. Add flour all at once; stirring rapidly. Cook and stir until mixture leaves sides of pan and gathers smoothly around spoon. Remove from heat. Add eggs one at a time; beat thoroughly after each. Keep beating until mixture looks satiny and breaks off when spoon is raised. Drop by spoonfuls on ungreased baking sheet, making 12 large or 18 medium mounds. Bake at 425° for 30 minutes or until puffed, dry and golden brown. Cool. Cut puffs part way through, crosswise. Fill with sweetened, vanilla-flavored whipped cream or Chocolate Filling.

CHOCOLATE FILLING:

1 pkg. (6 oz.) semi-sweet
  chocolate pieces
½ cup milk

¼ cup sugar
16 marshmallows (½ lb.)
1 teaspoon vanilla

1 cup whipping cream

Place chocolate pieces, milk, sugar and marshmallows in top of double boiler. Cook over hot water, stirring constantly, until mixture is smooth. Remove from heat; add vanilla; chill. Whip cream. Fold chocolate mixture into whipped cream. Fill cream puffs. If desired, frost tops with canned chocolate frosting, or sprinkle with confectioners' (powdered) sugar.

Cream Puff Dessert

Miniature Cream Puffs   1 quart vanilla ice cream
  (below)   1 quart raspberry sherbet
            Chocolate sauce, if desired

Make and cool miniature cream puffs. Place a layer of puffs
in 10-inch angel-food pan with removable bottom. Top with
layer of softened ice cream (1 quart). Repeat with layer of
puffs, then sherbet, then puffs. Freeze until firm, preferably overnight. Remove from freezer about 15 minutes before serving.
Remove from pan by running spatula around the outside edge
of mold and around tube; push bottom up and out of the tube
pan. With two large spatulas, one on each side of mold, lift from
bottom of pan; place on serving plate. Serve in slices with chocolate sauce, if desired.   *Makes 16 servings.*

MINIATURE CREAM PUFFS: Follow recipe for Cream Puffs
(p. 102). Drop by scant teaspoons on ungreased baking sheet.
Bake at 425° for about 15 minutes, or until puffed, dry and
golden brown. Remove from baking sheet with spatula; cool.
Makes about 90 to 100 puffs (miniature).

Eclairs

Follow recipe for Cream Puffs (p. 102). Drop rounded tablespoons about 2 inches apart in rows 6 inches apart on ungreased
baking sheets. With small spatula, spread each mound into a
rectangle about 4 inches long by 1-inch wide, rounding sides
and piling dough on top. Bake as directed for Cream Puffs. Cool
on racks. Cut eclairs in half, lengthwise and put together with
Cream Filling between halves. Spread tops with Caramel Glaze.
Makes about 18.

CREAM FILLING: Prepare 1 package vanilla pudding mix
(not instant) using 1½ cups milk instead of 2. Cool. Whip ½ cup
whipping cream; fold in.

CARAMEL GLAZE: Put ½ pound vanilla caramels in top of double boiler. Add ¼ cup water. Cook over boiling water, stirring often, until caramels melt and blend with water to make a smooth glaze. Spoon over tops of eclairs and spread thin.

CHOCOLATE ECLAIRS: Use chocolate pudding mix for filling. Frost with Chocolate Glaze.

CHOCOLATE GLAZE: Melt 2 squares (1 oz. each) unsweetened chocolate with 2 tablespoons each butter and hot water. Stir to blend. Stir in 1 to 1½ cups confectioners (powdered) sugar and ½ teaspoon vanilla. Beat until smooth. Spread thinly on eclairs.

BUTTERSCOTCH ECLAIRS: Use butterscotch pudding mix for filling. Frost with either Caramel or Chocolate Glaze. Sprinkle with chopped walnuts.

HAWAIIAN ECLAIRS: Use pineapple-cream pudding mix for filling. Frost with Vanilla Glaze.

VANILLA GLAZE: Blend 1½ cups confectioners' (powdered) sugar with 1 tablespoon soft butter or margarine, ⅛ teaspoon salt, ¼ teaspoon almond extract and 2½ tablespoons light cream. Spread thinly on eclairs. Sprinkle with chopped toasted almonds.

VIII. Candies and Confections

The recipes that follow are simple and uncomplicated—but they make delicious candies. An assortment of two or three, attractively packed, would be a charming hostess gift or a welcome bit of cheer for a shut-in.

Make up a few batches to have around for the holiday season, or for school vacations. Tuck two or three pieces in a lunch box for a surprise dessert. You'll find many happy uses for these easy-to-make sweets.

Santa's Sweets

2 pkgs. (6 oz. each) semi-sweet chocolate pieces
½ cup dairy sour cream
¾ cup confectioners' (powdered) sugar

¼ teaspoon salt
2 cups fine vanilla wafer crumbs
½ cup broken walnuts

Melt semi-sweet chocolate pieces over hot (not boiling) water. Remove from water, stir in sour cream, confectioners' (powdered) sugar and salt. Blend in vanilla wafer crumbs. Spread in foil-lined 8-inch square pan. Press walnuts into surface. Chill until firm. Cut into 1-inch squares. *Makes 64 pieces.*

Marzipan

1 pound canned almond
   paste
½ cup light corn syrup
1 jar (1 pint) marshmallow
   topping

2 teaspoons vanilla
6 cups sifted confectioners'
   (powdered) sugar
Food coloring

Combine almond paste, corn syrup, marshmallow topping and vanilla; mix thoroughly. Add sugar, 1 cup at a time, mixing well after each addition (knead in the last 2 or 3 cups with the hands) until marzipan is satiny. Mold small pieces into fruit or vegetable shapes. Insert tiny artificial leaves where needed while the marzipan is still soft. Let stand several hours to permit the surface to dry before painting. Paint with food coloring, diluted and mixed as necessary, using artist's brushes. Roll "potatoes" in a mixture of cocoa and cinnamon instead of painting. Roll "strawberries" and "raspberries" in red sugar after painting. Makes about 5 dozen pieces. Store in tightly covered metal boxes. Will keep indefinitely.

Jiffy Fudge

2 pkgs. (6 oz. each) semi-
   sweet chocolate pieces
¾ cup sweetened condensed
   milk
1 teaspoon vanilla

Melt semi-sweet chocolate pieces over hot (not boiling) water. Remove from heat; stir in milk and vanilla. Mix well. Turn into pan or shape as desired. Let stand several hours or overnight.

Makes about 1¼ pounds.

CHOCOLATE NUT SQUARES: Turn chocolate mixture into an 8-inch square pan. Cut into squares. Press whole almond or pecan or walnut half in each square.

PRALINES: Cool chocolate mixture thoroughly. Measure 1 tablespoon of mixture. Place on piece of waxed paper. Place another piece of waxed paper on top. Press with bottom of a water glass to make a 2-inch circle. Continue until all of chocolate mixture is used. Press pecans in center of each praline.

PEANUT OR COCONUT BALLS: Shape chocolate mixture into ¾-inch balls; roll in chopped peanuts or coconut.

CHOCOLATE NUT ROLLS: Add ½ cup coarsely chopped nuts to chocolate mixture. Divide mixture in half. Make 2 rolls about 1½ inches in diameter. Lightly press rolls into additional chopped nuts, covering all surfaces. Cut into 16 slices.

Marshmallow Walnut Fudge

½ cup miniature
    marshmallows
½ cup broken walnuts
2½ cups sugar
¾ cup evaporated milk
⅓ cup light corn syrup
2 tablespoons butter or
    margarine

1 large pkg. (12 oz.) or 2
    small pkgs. (6 oz. each)
    semi-sweet chocolate
    pieces
1 teaspoon vanilla
    Walnut halves, chopped
    walnuts, flaked coconut

Line an 8-inch square pan with aluminum foil. Cover bottom of pan with marshmallows and broken walnuts. Combine sugar, evaporated milk, corn syrup and butter in 3-quart saucepan. Bring to full, all-over boil, stirring constantly. Continue to boil 5 minutes, stirring constantly. Remove from heat. Add semi-sweet chocolate pieces and vanilla; stir until smooth. Pour ½ chocolate mixture into prepared pan. Let stand until cold; cut into squares. Turn remaining mixture onto greased cookie sheet; let stand until cool enough to handle. Grease hands and work additional butter or margarine (about 1 tablespoon) into fudge until smooth and pliable. Divide mixture into 4 parts and shape as follows: (1) Shape into 1½-inch patties and press walnut half on each patty; (2) Shape into cornucopias and press wide ends into chopped walnuts; (3) Shape into logs and roll in chopped walnuts; (4) Work in ¼ cup chopped walnuts and shape into 1-inch balls, roll in flaked coconut or chopped walnuts.

Makes approximately 2½ pounds.

Chocolate Marshmallows

1 envelope unflavored
gelatin
⅓ cup cold water
½ cup sugar
⅔ cup light corn syrup
1 teaspoon vanilla
3 squares (1 oz. each) unsweetened chocolate
¾ cup finely chopped peanuts

Soften gelatin in cold water; place over boiling water; stir until dissolved. Add sugar; stir until dissolved. Remove from heat. Place corn syrup and vanilla in large bowl of electric mixer. Add gelatin-sugar mixture; beat on highest speed until mixture becomes thick and of soft marshmallow consistency, about 15 minutes. While mixture is beating, melt chocolate; cool. When marshmallow consistency is reached, fold in cooled, melted chocolate by hand. Pour into greased pan, preferably about 7 x 10 x 1½ inches. Smooth off top with spoon or knife. Let stand in a cool place (not refrigerator) until well set, about 1 hour. To remove from pan, loosen around edges and invert on waxed paper. Cut into 1-inch squares with knife moistened with cold water. Roll in finely chopped peanuts. *Makes about 1½ pounds.*

Chocolate-Marshmallow Velvet

1 cup evaporated milk
2 cups sugar
2 pkgs. (6 oz. each) semi-sweet chocolate pieces
1 teaspoon vanilla
1½ cups miniature marshmallows

Combine evaporated milk and sugar in saucepan. Place over low heat; stir until sugar is dissolved and mixture comes to a boil. Increase heat; boil 2 minutes, stirring constantly. Remove from heat; add semi-sweet chocolate pieces and vanilla; stir until smooth. Turn about ½ the chocolate mixture into waxed-paper-lined 8-inch square pan. Cover with miniature marshmallows, pressing them gently into the chocolate. Top with remaining chocolate mixture. Chill. Cut into squares.

Cherry Pecan Logs

5 tablespoons evaporated milk, divided
½ teaspoon rum flavoring
2½ cups (about) sifted confectioners' (powdered) sugar

1 cup coarsely chopped candied cherries
14 vanilla caramels (¼ lb.)
1½ cups coarsely chopped pecans

Fondant base: Combine 2 tablespoons evaporated milk and rum flavoring in mixing bowl. Stir in sugar until blended; knead until smooth and shiny. To make logs: Knead in cherries, adding more sugar if necessary. Shape into two 6-inch logs; roll in waxed paper; chill until firm. Combine caramels and remaining 3 tablespoons evaporated milk; heat over boiling water until melted, stirring often. Turn caramel mixture into pie pan. Quickly roll logs in caramel mixture, then in pecans. Roll in waxed paper; chill until firm. Slice.

Chocolate Dipped Fruit

24 bite-size chunks fresh pineapple (about ¼ medium pineapple)
24 seedless grapes
2 ripe bananas, peeled and cut into 12 slices each

24 Bing cherries with stems
1 pkg. (12 oz.) or 2 pkgs. (6 oz. each) semi-sweet chocolate pieces
⅔ cup vegetable shortening (not oil)

Stick wooden picks or tiny metal skewers into pineapple chunks, grapes and banana slices. Place with cherries in a single layer in waxed-paper-lined shallow pan so that pieces do not touch. Place in freezer for 2 or more hours, until frozen solid. Put chocolate pieces and shortening in 2-cup measure (that's right—it all melts down to 2 cups and doesn't run over). Place cup in pan of hot (not boiling) water until melted; stir until smooth. Leave chocolate mixture in pan of hot water, but remove from heat. Dip pieces of frozen fruit into chocolate mixture to coat. Do not put fruit back in pan until coating hardens (the chocolate hardens almost immediately on frozen fruit). Cover pan with foil; return to freezer until ready to serve. Fruit is best served as soon as possible after dipping. Do not remove from freezer until ready to serve; fruit will thaw for eating in 5 to 12 minutes. *Makes 6 servings of 4 pieces of each fruit.*

Index